Abraham Booth

An Essay on the Kingdom of Christ

Abraham Booth

An Essay on the Kingdom of Christ

ISBN/EAN: 9783337184384

Printed in Europe, USA, Canada, Australia, Japan

Cover: Foto ©Lupo / pixelio.de

More available books at **www.hansebooks.com**

ESSAY

ON THE

KINGDOM

OF

CHRIST.

BY

ABRAHAM BOOTH.

THEY SHALL SPEAK OF THE GLORY OF THY
KINGDOM. *Pfalm* cxlv. 11.

NEW-YORK:

Printed and *Sold* by W. DURELL., at his
Book-Store and *Printing-Office,*
No. 19, QUEEN-STREET.
M,DCC,XCI.

PREFACE.

THE Kingdom of Chrift is a fubject of great importance: for, according to the views we have of that kingdom will our conclufions be, refpecting various branches of religious conduct. If thofe views be imaginary, thefe conclufions muft be falfe. By the former, the glory of Meffiah's regal character will be obfcured: by the latter, his worfhip will be corrupted: whereas the true doctrine concerning this holy empire, may not only be the mean of preferving from thofe evils, but of prefenting us with *data* for the decifion of many difputes among the profeffors of Chriftianity. A competent acquaintance, therefore, with its nature and laws, its emoluments and honors, is clofely connected with our duty and our happinefs: which acquaintance muft be derived from divine Revelation.

Important, however, as the subject manifestly is, it has been but seldom profeffedly difcuffed. This confideration was a leading motive to the prefent attempt. To illuftrate the nature of our Lord's Kingdom, and to infer the conclufions flowing from it, conftitute the defign of this Effay.

The author has expreffed his thoughts with great freedom ; yet without intending the leaft offence to any party of Chriftians, or to any perfon, from whofe notions and practices he confcientioufly differs. In the courfe of difcuffion he animadverts, indeed, on fome particulars, with a degree of feverity : but then they appear to him in the light of *political artifices*, which either impeach the dominion of Chrift in his own kingdom ; or degrade and corrupt that worfhip which he requires. Now, in cafes of this kind, the writer is of opinion, that allegiance to the King Meffiah, and true benevolence to man, demand the language of marked oppofition.

Such is the nature of our Lord's em-pire, that few of his loyal fubjects can ferioufly reflect upon it, without feel-ing themfelves both delighted and re-proved. *Delighted;* becaufe it is for the honor of their Mediator, to be the Sovereign of a fpiritual monarchy. A character of this kind apparently fuits the dignity of his Perfon, the defign of his mediation, and the riches of his grace.--*Reproved;* becaufe they daily find a want of that fpirituality in their affections, and of that heavenly mind-ednefs, which become the profeffed fubjects of fuch a kingdom. When meditating on the characteriftics of this holy empire, they ftand convicted be-fore its divine Sovereign of much car-nality and worldly mindednefs, over which they fincerely mourn: while

merely nominal subjects of the King
Messiah, or superficial professors of the
gracious gospel, are but little concerned about the state of their hearts, in reference to heaven ; or with regard to
the spirituality of their worship.

This being the case with multitudes,
the author would not be much surprised, were various particulars in the following pages to prove disgusting to the
taste of numbers professing godliness.
But facts are stubborn things ; and the
sayings of Jesus Christ must not be ex-
plained away, that conscience may rest
in a false peace, or that the public taste
may be gratified*. For, when thinking
of our Sublime Sovereign, THY KING-
DOM COME, is the language of every upright heart, let carnal professors and the
profligate world say what they please.

A. BOOTH.

Goodman's Fields, July 30, 1783.

* LUTHER says, Potius quam aliquid Regno
Christi et Gloriæ ejus decedat, ruat non solum pax
sed cœlum et terra. *Loci Commun.* Class iv. p 55.

A N

E S S A Y

ON THE

KINGDOM of CHRIST.

IT having been revealed by ancient Prophets, that the Lord Meffiah fhould be a King, and have univerfal empire, the chofen tribes in every age expected his appearance under the regal character. While, however, the general idea of that expectation was fully warranted by the Spirit of prophecy, the bulk of Abraham's natural pofterity were under a grofs miftake, refpecting the true defign of their Meffiah's appearance, and the real nature of his kingdom: which miftake had the moft pernicious influence upon their temper and conduct, when the gracious promife of his coming was fulfilled.

The fenfe which they affixed to prophecies refpecting the great Redeemer, was manifeftly fuch as flattered their pride and foftered their carnality. This gave it a decided advantage, in their eitimation, over that for which eur Lord and his Apoftles contended; and led them to overlook whatever in the ancient Oracles oppofed their fecular views. Ignorant of their fpiritual wants, and flufhed with a falfe perfuafion of intereft in Jehovah's peculiar favor, on the ground of carnal defcent from Abraham, and of the Covenant made at Horeb; the doctrine, example, and claims of Chrift, were extremely offenfive. Not appearing as a temporal prince, dilcovering no difpofition to free them from the Roman yoke, and frequently addreffing their confciences with keen reproof, on account of their pride and hypocrify, fuperftition and covetoufnefs; they rejected with determined oppofition all the evidences of his divine miffion, treated him as an impoftor, and procured his crucifixion.-- After he was rifen from the dead, and afcended to heaven, multitudes of them indeed believed, and profeffed the Chriftian faith : but a great majority of the nation continued in hardened impenitence, and perfecuted the Apoftles with unrelenting malevolence. Thus they proceeded till, divine forbearance being exhaufted, *wrath came upon them to the uttermoft*, in the total fubverfion of their civil and ecclefiaftical polity.

This miftake of the Jews, refpecting the kingdom of their Meffiah, lying at the foundation of all the oppofition with which they treated him, and of their own ruin ; it behoves us to guard with diligence againft every thing which tends to fecularize the dominion of Chrift : left, by corrupting the Gof-pel Oeconomy, we difhonor the Lord Redeemer, and be finally punifhed as the enemies of his government. Our danger of contracting guilt, and of in-curring divine ~~judg~~ment in this way, is far from fmall. For we are fo con-verfant with fenfible objects, and fo de-lighted with exterior fhow, that we are naturally inclined to wifh for fomething in the religion of Jefus, to gratify our carnality. Under the influence of that mafter prejudice, *the expectation of a temporal kingdom*, Jewifh depravity re-jected Chrift ; and our corruption, if we be not watchful, may fo mifrepre-fent his empire, and oppofe his royal prerogatives, as implicitly to fay, *We will not have him to rule over us.*

Among the numerous admirable fay-ings of Jefus Chrift, and of his Apoftles, that ftand recorded in the New Tefta-ment, and are adapted to inftruct us in this important fubject ; there is one which deferves peculiar notice. The faying to which I advert, is part of that *good confeffion* which our Lord witneffed before Pontius Pilate ; *My kingdom is not of this world.* A concife, but comprehenfive declaration, and worthy of him that made it !--This capital faying may be confidered as the grand maxim on which he formed his conduct when among men ; and it is pregnant with needful inftruction to all his difciples, refpecting the New Oeconomy and the Chriftian Church Relative to matters of that kind, there is not, perhaps, a more interefting paffage in all the New Teftament ; nor one which is better adapted to rebuke the pride and carnality of millions who bear the Chriftian character. To approve of Chrift as a fpiritual monarch, agreeably to the meaning and tendency of this emphatical text, requires a degree of heavenly mindednefs which comparatively few poffefs.

My kingdom is not of this world, fays Meffiah the Prince, when ftanding before the Roman governor, and queftioned about his claim of dignity. He boldly avows himfelf a King ; yet, while advancing his title to the honors, of royalty, he tacitly informs Pilate that the civil rights of Cefar had nothing to fear from him; and that his own difciples had no advantages to expect, of a fecular kind, as the refult of embarking in his caufe.----Our Lord, a little while before, had implicitly conveyed the general idea of this declaration, by receiving from a furrounding multitude the acclamations due to his royal character, when *riding upon an afs*: for while he accepted the honours of royalty, the poverty and meannefs of his appearance plainly implied, that his kingdom was not of a temporal kind.   Zechariah had foretold that the children of Zion fhould loudly rejoice in this humble manifestation of the King Meffiah, and that their joy fhould kindle into rapture. An incontrovertible evidence that he predicted the public inauguration of a Sovereign, whofe *kingdom is not of this world*.   For the loyal and affectionate fubjects of a political monarch never thought it matter of exultation, that he appeared among them, when proclaimed king, with all the marks of meannefs and of poverty.   Yet fo it was in refpect of the King Meffiah.

It is generally allowed, if I miftake
not, that the kingdom ot Chrift is no
other th\n the Golpel Church*; which
is both diftinguifhed from the worlc,
and oppoled to it. Relative to this
kingdom, and its divine Sovereign, Jehovah lays; *I have let my King upon my
holy hill of Zion.* This prophetic Oracle
was tulfilled when our Lord, *leading
captivity captive,* afcended on high and
fat down on the right of the eternal Father. Then was he moft folemnly in-
augurated and proclaimed King of the
New Teftament Church, amidft adoring myraids of attendant angels, and
fpirits of juft men made perfeÆ. In pur-
fuance of which moft grand invefliture
with his regal office, he diftributed
royal donatives, at the feaft of Pentecoft,
among his devoted fubjeÆts-- fuch donatives, as perfeÆly fuited the majefty
of his Perfon, and the nature of his
kingdom. Yes, that wonderful affem-
blage of fpiritual gifts and heavenly
graces, which he beftowed upon his
difciples at the Jewifh feftival, was a

* Regnum Dei in evangelia, fays WITSIUS. vix
alia fignificatione venit qua ., ut notet flatum exi-
mium et vere iherum Ecclefiæ Teftamenti Novi
fub Rege Meffia Exercitat, in Orat. Dominic.
Exercit, ix. § 11.

glorious firſt-fruit of his aſcenſion, and of his being *a prieſt upon his throne.* The Goſpel Church, which is the ſubject of his laws, the ſeat of his government, and the object of his care, being ſurrounded with powerful oppoſers ; he is repreſented as ruling *in the midſt of his enemies.* Nor ſhall his mediatorial kingdom and adminiſtration ceaſe, till all thoſe enemies become his ſootſtool.

The empire of Chriſt, indeed, extends to every creature : for *all authority in heaven and on earth* is in his hands, and he *is head over all things to the Church.* But the kingdom of which we treat, ſtands diſtinguiſhed from that of general Providence, as well as from every political ſtate. It muſt be conſidered, therefore, as conſiſting of thoſe perſons whom he bought with his blood, whom he calls by his grace, and over whom he reigns as a ſpiritual monarch. Theſe conſtitute what is frequently called, the Catholic Church, wherever the favored individuals may reſide. Of ſuch alſo, or of thoſe who make a credible profeſſion of being ſuch, all thoſe particular churches conſiſt, which conſtitute our Lord's viſible kingdom--that kingdom of which we ſpeak. Into the

B

principal characteriſtics of this holy empire, and into the genuine conſequences of thoſe criteria, we ſhall now enquire.

The Goſpel Church is a kingdom not of this world, in regard to its origin. From the time of Nimrod to the preſent age, ſecular empires have generally originated in the vile paſſions of their firſt founders : for, in almoſt every inſtance, avarice and pride, ambition and a luſt of dominion, have been conſpicuous.-- Not ſo, in the kingdom of Chriſt. The remote foundation of his dominion was laid in the counſels of Heaven before time commenced, by all comprehending wiſdom and infinite goodneſs, for the glory of God and the benefit of man : and the immediate baſis on which it ſtands, is his own vicarious obedience to divine law ; both as to its precepts, and as to its penalty. Juſtice and goodneſs, therefore, are the foundation of his throne. Mercy and truth attend the whole of his adminiſtration.

The kingdom of Chriſt is not of this world, reſpecting the ſubjects of his righteous government The generality of people in all countries, were *born* ſubjects of thofe governments under which they lived. No fooner, for inftance, were we capable of reflecting upon our civil connections, than we found ourfelves freeborn fubjects of the Britifh crown : and thus it commonly is in the fovereignties of fecular princes. Their dominion being confined to the exterior of human conduct, and not reaching the heart ; natural birth and local circumftances conftitue fubjects of the ftate, put them under the protection of law, and inveft them with civil rights. Such fubjects are perfectly well fuited to the kingdoms of this world, and to the character of their fovereigns. For, confidered as men, kings and fubjects are on a level : and, as diftinguifhed by political characters, their obligations are mutual ; allegiance on the one part, and protection on the other.----Befides, temporal kingdoms refpect the prefent world. The mutual duties of fovereigns and of fubjects, as fuch, regard the happinefs of civil fociety, and of that only. As an inveftiture with political fovereignty does not conftitute a lord of confcience, it gives no claim to authority in fpiritual things, but is entirely confined to the concerns of this world. It is, indeed, the indifpenfable duty of fecular princes, and of their people, to love and adore God . yet that obligation does not arife from any political relation fubfifting among them, but from their being reafonable creatures.   It is alfo their happinefs to be the fubjects of Jefus Chrift: but that felicity does not refult from any thing fhort of divine mercy exercifed upon them, as depraved and guilty creatures.

The kingdom and claims of Chrift being very different from thofe of Cefar, the qualifications and obedience of his real fubjects muft be fo too.   For perfons may be good fubjects of a temporal fovereign, and enjoy the rights of fuch a character, while they are fo far from bearing true allegiance to Jefus Chrift, as to be quite inimical to his dominion, and entire ftrangers to the privileges of his kingdom. The empire of Chrift *is not of this world :* it is not a temporal, but a fpiritual kingdom.   Our Lord, therefore, is a fpiritual fovereign ; whofe dominion extends to the mind, confcience, and heart, no lefs than to the external behaviour.   Confequently, all the fubjects of his government muft have fpiritual difpofitions, and yield fpiritual

obedience---- obedience, proceeding
from an enlightened underftanding, an
awakened confcience, and a renewed
heart. For, as is the fovereign, fuch
are the fubjeéts, and fuch the allegiance
required. A fpiritual Sovereign,
and fubjeéts yielding an obedience
merely external, are manifeftly incon-
fiftent.

As all mankind are born in a ftate of
apoftafy from God : as the natural turn
of the heart, or *the carnal mind, is not-
fubjeét to the law of God, neither indeed
can be*; we muft be born again---*born,
not of blood, nor of the will of the flefh, nor
of the will of man, but of God*, before we
are permitted to confider ourfelves, or
to be confidered by others, as the fubjeéts of Him whofe kingdom is of a
fpiritual kind. Remarkable are the
words of our Lord, when fpeaking of
his loyal fubjeéts : *They are not of the
world, even as I am not of the world*. No :
they are defcribed by the Apoftles, as
being *of the truth; of faith;* and *of
God** *Of the truth :* enlightened,
converted, and fanétified by the gofpel.
Of faith : living by it; deriving peace.

B 2

* John xviii. 17. Gal. iii. 7, 9, 1, Joh. iv. 46.

and holinefs from Jefus Chrift through
believing in him. *Of God:* born of
him ; or *begotten again to a lively hope,
by the refurrection of Jefus Chrift from
the dead.*----Such are the fubjects of
our Lord's kingdom : in oppofition to
whom, the New Teftament reprefents
the reft of our apoftate race, as being *of
the works of the law; of the world; of
darknefs ;* and *of the devil**. *Of the
works of the law ;* feeking acceptance
with God by their own imperfect obedience, which leaves them under a
curfe. *Of the world* : carnally minded,
and in a ftate of enmity to God. *Of
darknefs* : ignorant of their perifhing
ftate, and unacquainted with Jefus
Chrift. *Of the devil*: partakers of his
image, fubjects of his dominion, and
performers of his will†. So great is
the contraft formed by Scripture, between thofe who are under our Lord's
government, and the reft of mankind !
Agreeably to which, real Chriftians are
further defcribed, as *delivered from the
power of darknefs,* or the tyranny of
Satan, and tranflated into the kingdom

* Gal. iii 10 Joh. viii. 23 1 Joh iv 5. 1 Theff.
v. 5. Joh viii, 38, 41. 44 1 Joh. lii. 8 12 † Rom.
viii, 6, 7, 8. Eph. v, 8, Joh. viii. 44. Eph. ii. 2.

of God's dear Son : and as being *of God*, while all the reft of the *world lies in wickedneſs.* None, therefore, but thofe who are born from above, are the fubjects of Jeſus Chriſt : for if the heart be not under his dominion, he reigns not at all as a fpiritual monarch.

That none but real Chriſtians are fub- jects of our Lord's kingdom, is yet further apparent from the defcriptive characters of thofe that were members of the apoftolic churches. We find them defcribed in the New Teſtament, as *gladly receiving the word* of grace, as *the called of Jeſus Chriſt*, and as *called to be faints.* The Apoſtles denominate them *brethren, faithful brethren, holy brethren, faints,* and *lively ſtones* in the fpiritual temple*. Thefe and fimilar characters are frequently applied to members of the primitive churches in general ; and of thofe churches the vi- fible kingdom of Chriſt then ccnfiſted. We may therefore fay, with VITRINGA ; " The kingdom of grace, in which " Chriſt is king upon mount Zion, is " properly and emphatically *the king-*

---

* Acts ii. 41. Rom. i 6. 1 Cor. i. 2. Eph. i. 1. Philip. i. 1. Col. i. 2. 2 Theff. i 3. Heb. iii. 1. 1 Pet. 1. 2, 3, and ii. 5. 2 Pet. i. 1,

" *dom of Chrift :* of which none are
" fubjects, except thofe who are cho-
" fen, called, faithful, peaceable, and
" humble ; in whom Jefus Chrift lives
" by his Spirit, as in the members of
" a myftical and fpiritual body, of
" which he is the head*."

This view of our Lord's fubjects is
perfectly agreeable to the nature and
genius of the New Covenant, with
which the Meffiah's kingdom is clofely
connected : becaufe it appears, that
fubjects of any other defcription, have
no reafon to confider themfelves as
covenantees ; and it is plain that a divine Covenant muft fuit the Kingdom,
to which it belongs, whether Jewifh
or Chriftian.---When, *in'the fulnefs of
time,* God performed his gracious and
comprehenfive promife of bleffing all
nations, it was by the intervention of
a New and better Covenant than that,
which was made at Sinai.. For thus
it is written : *Behold, the days come,
faith the Lord, that I will make a New
Covenant with the houfe of Ifrael, and
with the houfe of Judah :* NOT ACCORD-
ING TO THE COVENANT THAT I MADE

* *Obfervat. Soc.* L V. C. iv. † 8. See Dr.
ERSKINE's *Theolog. Differtat.* p, 111—115.

WITH THEIR FATHERS, IN THE DAY THAT I TOOK THEM BY THE HAND TO BRING THEM OUT OF THE LAND OF EGYPT ; *which my Covenant they brake although I was an hufband unto them, faith the Lord. But this fhall be the Covenant that I will make with the houfe of Ifrael, After thofe days, faith the Lord, I will put my law in their inward parts, and write it in their hearts, and will be their God, and they fhall be my people. And they fhall teach no more every man his neighbour, and every man his brother, faying, Know the Lord: for they fhall all know me, from the leaft of them unto the greateft of them, faith the Lord : for I will forgive their iniquity, and I will remember their fin no more**.

This admirably gracious Covenant is completely fuited to a fpiritual kingdom, and to the fubjects we have been defcribing : for it announces no defigns, makes no provifions, confers no bleffings, but thofe that are fpiritual, internal, and everlafting. The true knowledge of Jehovah, writing his law in the heart, forgivenefs of all fin, and perpetual relation to God, are

---

* Jer. xxxi. 31—34. Heb. viii. 8, 9.

the bleffings for which it engages;
but there is not a word refpecting
temporal bleffings, nor concerning any
merely *external relation* to the Great
Supreme, though thefe were *the grand
articles* in the Covenant made at Horeb.
Covenantees, therefore, under the
Chriftian Oeconomy, can be no other
than the fpiritual feed of Abraham:
and fuch are the fubjects of this kingdom. Hence the Gofpel Covenant is
called *new*, and is exprefsly oppofed
to the Sinai Confederation, from which
it is extremely different. It is alfo
pronounced *a better* Covenant than
that which Jehovah made with the
ancient Ifrael : and fo it is, whether
we confider its objects, its bleffings,
its confirmation, or its continuance.
Its *objects :* for they are the fpiritual
feed of Abraham, gathered out of all
nations. Its *bleffings :* for they are all
fpiritual and internal. Its *confirmation :*
for it was ratified by the death of Chrift.
Its *continuance :* for it is *an everlafling
Covenant, ordered in all things and fure.*
Yes, it is as much better than the
Covenant made at Sinai, as being the
children of God by regeneration, is
preferable to carnal defcent from A-
braham---as the number of God's elect

in all nations, exceeds that of the chofen tribes---as bleſſings entiiely ſpiritual and immortal, are more excel-
lent than thoſe of an earthly kind and
of ſhort duration---as redemption from
ſpiritual bondage and eternal ruin, is
greater and nobler than deliverance
from temporal ſlavery---as the ratifi-
cation of this Covenant, by the blood
of Immanuel, is more ſacred than that
which the Old Covenant received by
the ſlaughter of brute animals---as the
Son of God, the mediator of it, is
greater than Moſes, who appeared
under that character at Horeb---and
as a Covenant of everlaſting efficacy,
that ſecures the final happineſs of all
to whom it relates, is better than one
of a temporary nature, which was vi-
olated by the covenantees, and is become for ever obſolete. Hence we
read, not only of a better *teſtament*,
but alſo of better *promiſes*, on which
the New Covenant is eſtabliſhed ; of a
better *hope*, introduced by it ; of better *ſacrifices*, by which guilt is expiated ;
of better *things* provided for the Chriſtian, than were enjoyed by the Jewiſh
church ; and of a better *country* for
an inheritance*, than the earthly Ca-

* Heb. viii. 6. vii. 19. ix. 23. xi. 17. 40.

naan, Nay, we are affured by an infpired writer, that the Sinai Covenant
and the Mofaic Difpenfation had no
glory attending them, compared with
that of the New Covenant and of the
Meffiah's Oeconomy*. Now, to this
more glorious Covenant, the kingdom
of Chrift, and the fubjects of it, muft a-
gree. As, therefore, none but fpiritual
bleffings are contained in that Covenant; fo none but real faints are the
fubjects of our Lord's dominion.

Very different, then, is the kingdom
of Chrift from the ancient *Ifraelifh
Theocracy.* For, of that Theocracy,
all Abraham's natural defcendents were
true fubjects, and properly qualified
members of the Jewifh church; fuch
only excepted, as had not been circum-
cifed according to the order of God,
or were guilty of fome capital crime.
To be an obedient fubject of their civil government, and a complete member in their ecclefiaftical ftate, were
manifeftly the fame thing; becaufe, by
treating Jehovah as their political
fovereign, they avowed him as the true
God, and were entitled to all the emoluments of their National Covenant.

* 2 Cor. iii. 7—11,

Under that Oeconomy, Jehovah acknowledged all thofe for *his people*, and himfelf as *their God*, who performed an external obedience to his commands, even though in their hearts difaffected to him*. Thefe prerogatives were enjoyed, independent of fanctifying grace, and of any pretention to it, either in themfelves, or in their parents.

The ftate of things, however, under the New Oeconomy, is extremely different. For the great Proprietor and Lord of the Chriftian church, having abfolutely difclaimed a kingdom that is *of this world*, cannot acknowledge any as the fubjects of his government, who do not know and revere him--who do not confide in him, and fincerely love him. Having entirely laid afide thofe enfigns of political fovereignty, and thofe marks of external grandeur, which made fuch a fplendid appearance in the Jewifh Theocracy ; he difdains to be called *the King*, or *the God*, of any perfon who does not obey and *worfhip him in fpirit and in truth*. Appearing as the head of his church, merely under the

C

* Judges viii. 23. 1 Sam. viii 6, 7. and xii. 12.
2 Chron, xxviii. 5. xxix. 23. 2 Chron. ix. 8.

character of a spiritual monarch, over whomsoever he reigns, it is in the understanding, by the light of his truth; in the conscience, by the force of his authority; and in the heart, by the influence of his love : for as to all others, his dominion is that of Providence, not that of Grace.--The New Testament affords no more ground for concluding, that our being descended from parents of a certain description, constitutes us the subjects of our Lord's kingdom; than it does to suppose, that carnal descent, in a particular line of ancestry, confers a claim to the character and work of ministers in the same kingdom.

It is of great importance to the right interpretation of many passages in the Old Testament, that this particular be well understood and kept in view. Jehovah is very frequently represented as the LORD and GOD of all the ancient Israelites; even where it is manifest that multitudes of them were considered as destitute of internal piety, and many of them as enormously wicked. How, then, could he be called *their* Lord, and *their* God, in distinction from his relation to Gentiles, (whose creator, benefactor, and sovereign he was) except on the ground of the Sinai Cove-

nant ? He was THEIR *Lord*, as being the
fovereign whom, by a federal tranfaction, they were bound to obey, in oppofition to every political monarch, who
fhould at any time prefume to govern
them by laws of his own. He was THEIR
God, as the only object of holy worfhip; and whom, by the fame National
Covenant, they had folemnly engaged
to ferve according to his own rule, in
oppofition to every Pagan idol. But
that National relation between Jehovah
and Ifrael being long fince diffolved,
and the Jew having no prerogative
above the Gentile; the nature of the
Gofpel Oeconomy, and the Meffiah's
kingdom, abfolutely forbids our fuppofing, that either Jews or Gentiles are
warranted to call the Great Supreme
THEIR *Lord*, or THEIR *God*, if they do
not yield willing obedience to him, and
perform fpiritual worfhip. It is, therefore, either for want of underftanding,
or of confidering, the nature, afpect,
and influence of the Sinai Conftitution,
that many perfons dream of the New
Covenant, in great numbers of places,
where Mofes and the Prophets had no
thought about it; but had the Conven-
tion at Horeb directly in view. It is
owing to the fame ignorance, or inad-

vertency, that others argue from various passages in the Old Testament, for justification before God by their own obedience, and against the final perseverance of real saints. Because, to be entitled to national happiness, by performing the conditions of the Sinai Covenant, and to lose that right by backsliding into profligacy of manners; are very different things, from obtaining justification before God, and forfeiting an interest in the great Redeemer--so different, that there is no arguing from the one to the other.

Again: As none but real Christians are the subjects of our Lord's kingdom, neither adults, nor infants, can be members of the Gospel Church, in virtue of an *external* covenant, or of a *relative* holiness. A striking disparity this, between the Jewish and the Christian church. Of this difference we may be assured by considering, That a barely relative sanctity, supposes its possessors to be the people of God in a merely external sense: that such an external people, supposes an external covenant, or one that relates to exterior conduct and temporal blessings: and an external covenant supposes an external king. Now an external king, is a political fovereign : but fuch is not our Lord Jefus Chrift, nor yet the divine Father. Once, indeed, it was otherwife: for, concerning the Ifraelitifh nation, it is thus written ; *I, Jehovah, will be thy king. Gideon faid unto them, I will not rule over you, neither fhall my fon rule over you. Jehovah fhall rule over you. Jehovah, your God, was your king**.-It was the peculiar honor and happinefs of Ifrael, to have a Sovereign who was the only object of their worfhip. For thus the Pfalmift fings ; *Bleffed is the nation, whofe* (king) JEHOVAH *is their God†!* Hence Jehovah's complaint ; *They have rejected me, that I fhould not reign over them‡.* Yes, Jehovah, as a temporal monarch, ftood related to the ancient Ifraelites, and entered into a federal tranfaction with them at Sinai, not only as the Object of their worfhip, but as their King. their judicial and civil infti-tutes, their laws of war and of peace, various orders refpecting the land they occupied, and the annual acknow-ledgments to the great Proprietor of

C 2

---

* Hofea xiii. 10. Judges viii. 23   1 Sam. xii, 12.
† Pf. xxxiii. 12 and cxliv. 15. *Heb.* See the Sep-tuagint Verfion, and that of JUNIUS and TRE-MELLIUS; together with POLI *Synopf.* and VA-NEME *Comment.* in loc.   ‡ 1 Sam. viii. 7.

it, were all from God, as their political sovereign. Hence all the natural posterity of Abraham were Jehovah's people, on the ground of an external covenant made with the whole nation. The children of Israel, being distinguished from the Gentile world, by a system of ceremonial precepts, and their divine Sovereign residing among them, were denominated *a holy nation :* for that external sanctity which they possessed, seems to have arisen, partly from their *National Covenant,* and partly from their having *the Divine Presence,* among them. By the former, they renounced idolatry in all its forms, and gave up themselves to Jehovah in opposition to the false objects of Pagan worship ; which separation to the service of God, is denominated *holiness.* By the latter, they had a kind of local nearness to God, which conferred a relative sanctity ; as appears by various instances. When, for example, Moses with astonishment beheld the burning bush, the ground on which he stood was pronounced *holy,* because of Jehovah's peculiar presence there. Thus it was in the case of Joshua: and so in regard to the place of our Lord's transfiguration ; for Peter calls it *the* HOLY

mount*. And why was part of the ancient fanctuary called *the moft holy place?*
but becaufe Jehovah in a fingular manner, and under a vifible emblem, dwelt
there. Hence it is manifeft, that the
Divine Prefence, whether under the
form of an *auguft perfonage*, as in the
cafe of Jofhua; or under the emblem
of *devouring fire*, as in the bufh, and upon mount Sinai†; or under the milder
appearance of *a luminous cloud*, as over
the mercy feat, and at our Lord's transfiguration, confers a relative holinefs.
It is alfo equally plain, that this miraculous prefence of God being with-
drawn from the feveral places to which
we have juft adverted, they have now
no more holinefs than any other part of
the earth.

So the Ifraelites, being feparated
from all other nations for the worfhip
of Jehovah as their God, to the exclufion of all idolatry; avowing fubjection
to him as their king, in contradiftincti-
onto all other fovereigns; and he refi-
ding among them in the fanctuary, as
in his royal palace; there was a rela-

tive holinefs attending their perfons, and almoſt every thing pertaining to them. For not only Jehovah's royal pavilion, with all its utenfils and fer-vices; the miniſters of that fanctuary and their feveral veftments; but the people in general, the metropolis of their country, the houfes of indivi-duals, the land cultivated by them, and the produce of that land, were all ſtiled *holy**.---The Divine Prefence re-fiding among them, appears to have had an extenfive influence upon the people, with regard to relative fanc-tity and external purity. So, in cafes of corporal pollution by difeafe, the patients were to be excluded from the common intercourfes of fociety, that they might not defile the camp, in the midſt of which their fublime Sovereign dwelt†. Nay, divine law exprefsly required, that even the furface of the ground on which they trod ſhould be preferved from one fpecies of defile-ment; and the injunction is enforced by this confideration, *For Jehovah thy God walketh in the midſt of the camp*‡.

* See Exod xxviii. 2, 4 xxix. 1. Lev xix. 23, 24. xx. 26 xxv 2, 4. xxvii. 14, 30. Numb. xvi. 3, 38. xxxv. 34. Deut. vii. 6   † Numb. v. 2, 3. and xxxv. 34. ‡ Deut. xxiii. 12, 13, 14

Remarkably to our purpofe is the declaration of God, when fpeaking of the ancient fanctuary; *There I will meet with the children of Ifrael, and* Ifrael (not *the tabernacle*) *fhall be fanctified by my glory.**. For, as VENEMA ob-ferves, " neither the *tabernacle* nor the
" *altar*, is to be underftood; but the
" *Ifraelites themfelves*, as appears by
" the connection and feries of the
" difcourfe. Becaufe, in the imme-
" diately following verfe, the fancti-
" fication of the tabernacle, and of
" the altar, is exprefsly mentioned.
" Befides, it is plain that the external
" fymbol of Jehovah's prefence, was
" a fufficient indication of God's *glory*
" in the tabernacle. Thus the holinefs
" of the people, equally as that of
" places, was derived from the ex-
" ternal prefence of God†."---Now, as the Divine Prefence had a local, vi-fible refidence over the mercy-feat, which was the throne of Jehovah; as that Prefence among the Ifraelites had fuch an extenfive operation upon their ftate, both in refpect of privilege and of duty; as the whole nation was a

* Exod. xxix, 43. Vid. JUNIUM and TREMELL. in loc.
† Differtat. Sac. L. ii. C. iii. § 6.

typical people, and a great part of their worship of a shadowy nature ; we need not wonder, that in such an ecclesiastico-political kingdom almost every thing should be esteemed, in a relative sense, *holy*.

Under the Gospel Dispensation, however, these peculiarities have no existence. For Christ has not made an external covenant with any people. He is not the king of any particular nation. He dwells not in a palace made with hands. His throne is in the heavenly sanctuary ; nor does he afford his visible Presence in any place upon earth. The partition wall between Jews and Gentiles has long been demolished : and, consequently, our divine Sovereign does not stand related to any people, or to any person, so as to confer a relative sanctity, or to produce an external holiness

While the Sinai Covenant continued in force, the Son of God was the King of the Jews : for though, by Saul and others bearing the regal character, the Divine government was obscured, yet it was not abolished. The kingdom of Israel, *in the hands of the Sons of David*, being denominated *the king-dom of Jehovah;* the throne on which Solomon fat being called *the throne of Jehovah** ; and the laws of the ftate being ftill divine, we are led to view the Jewifh kings as the *vicegerents* of Jeho-vah†.---In this light the queen of She-ba confidered Solomon when fhe faid ; *Bleffed be the Lord thy God, which de-lighted in thee to fet the* ʘn HIS THRONE, *to be king* FOR THE LORD THY GOD‖. Of the Jewifh magiftrates it is alfo written, *Ye judge not for man, but for Jehovah§.* Now fo long as a political relation fubfifted between the Son of God and the feed of Abraham, an exter-nal holinefs continued, as refulting from that relation. But though this foundation of relative fanctity was not removed till the death of Chrift, there is no intimation in the Evangeli-cal Hiftory of any one being entitled to a New Teftament rite, or to the cha-racter of a fubject in the Meffiah's kingdom, in virtue of that holinefs.

---

* 2. Chron. xiii. 8. 1 Chron. xxiii. 5. and xxix. 23 † Vid. WITSII Mifcell. Sac. Tom. II p 920—936. VENEMAE. *Hift. Ecclef. Vet. Teft.* Tom. I. ‡198. *Differtat, Sac.* L. II. C. iv. § 2 Chron. ix. 8

Nay, the reverfe appears in the conduct
of John toward the Jews*.

The Covenant made at Horeb having
long been obfolete, all its peculiarities
are vanifhed away : among which, relative fanctity made a confpicuous
figure. That National Conftitution
being abolifhed, Jehovah's political fovereignty is at an end. The covenant
therefore now in force, and the royal
relation of our Lord to the church, are
entirely fpiritual. All that external
holinefs of perfons, of places, and of
things, which exifted under the Old
Oeconomy, is gone for ever : fo that if
the profeffors of Chriftianity do not
poffefs a real, internal fanctity, they
have none at all.---The National Confederation at Sinai is exprefsly contrafted, in holy Scripture, with the New
Covenant† : and though the latter manifeftly provides for internal holinefs,
refpecting all the covenantees, yet it
fays not a word about relative fanctity.
And, indeed, how fhould it ? fince, by
its commencement, the whole Sinai
Conftitution became obfolete ; the

* 2 Chron. xix. 6. § Matt. iii. 7—12. † Jer.
xxxi. 31—34. Heb. viii. 7—13.

partition wall was broken down; the special relation between God and A-braham's natural seed ceafed, and left no difference of a religious kind between Jews and Gentiles---no difference, in refpect of nearnefs to God and communion with him, except that which regeneration and faith in Chrift produce. For, under the prefent Difpenfation, *Chrift is all in all.* We may therefore fafely conclude, that were the Jews converted and re-fettled in Paleftine, both they and their infant offspring would be as entirely deftitute of the ancient relative holi-nefs, as thofe Mahommedans are who now refide in that country.

But did an external holinefs now exift, we fhould be obliged to confider it as very different from that of the ancient Ifraelites : for it appears, by what has been faid, that the grounds of their exterior fanctity make no part of the Chriftian Oeconomy. Befides, their holinefs extended to the whole nation : but in what Utopia fhall we find all the inhabitants poffeffed of this relative purity ? Theirs continued as long as they lived ; except they com-

D

mitted some enormous crime, by which
they forfeited their lives, or were cast
out of the congregation. for it did
not wear out by age, nor was it lost
merely by continuing in a state of un-
regeneracy. Whereas, that external
holiness for which so many plead, is
not generally considered by them as
extending beyond the time of infancy.
---But why should any contend for the
relative holiness of infants, who deny
a sanctity of that kind, to places of
worship, clerical habits, and various
other things ? for it is plain that the
Jewish external purity, whether of
persons, of places, or of things, originated in the same National Covenant, and in the same relation of God
to Israel : and, consequently, must
have the same duration in one case, as
in another. We may therefore justly
conclude, that the federal and relative
holiness of which so many speak, neither agrees with the laws of Judaism,
nor with the nature of Christianity.
But if so, it cannot belong to the
kingdom of Christ.

Further : If all the subjects of Christ
be real saints, it may be justly queried
whether any *National religious esta-*

blifhment can be a part of his kingdom. That multitudes of individuals belonging to fuch eftablifhments are fubjects of the King Mefliah, is cheerfully granted : but is it not plain, that a National church is inimical to the fpirit of our Lord's declaration. *My kingdom is not of this world?* Does not that comprehenfive and important faying compel us to view the church and the world in a *contrafted* point of light? And does not the idea of a National church lead us to *confound* them? Does it not manifeftly confound *the church of the firft-born, which are written in heaven;* with *the world, that lies in wickednefs,.* whofe names are entered in parifh regifters* ?---The fubjects of

---

* It has been well obferved by a fenfible writer, that when Jefus told Pilate "the fole end of his
" kingdom and of his coming into the world, was
" *truth* and the propagation of it ; Pilate fays,
" *What is truth?* He knew very well that *truth* had
" little or nothing to do with the maxims of
" wordly policy : that he, that is Jefus, was not
" at all likely to be a competitor with Cæfar:
" that a *kingdom of truth* could not interfere with
" the claims of his mafter: that it was trifling
" to accufe him as an enemy to Cæfar. But
" then, had Jefus faid that he was fetting upon a
" kingdom that claimed an aliance with the ftate,
" and which pretended to a fupremacy, Pilate

our Lord's kingdom are born of God,
are called out of the world; but natural birth and local circumftances are
confidered, either as giving memberfhip, or as entitling to a pofitive rite
which confers memberfhip, in a National church. The Church of England, for inftance, includes all Englifh
fubjects of the Britifh crown, whether
they be moral or profligate, pious or
profane : fuch only excepted, as have
not been baptized, or as lie under a
fentence of excommunication. Nay,
fo tenacious is the Englifh Church of
this idea, as to confider numbers within its pale, who never confidered themfelves in that light. For, in certain
cafes, well known to the doctors in
Canon Law, Proteftant Diffenters, and
even Popifh recufants, are caft out of
its communion---*caft out*, with dread-
ful penalties annexed, though they
never acknowledged themfelves to
be *in!*

The Church of England, indeed, is
manifeftly a fecular kingdom. For it

" would have had whereof to accufe him." *Comment on Bp.* WARBURTON's *Alliance between Church
and State,* p. 9.

is eftablifhed by human laws, and ac-
knowledges a political head : nor is it
efteemed material whether that head
be male or female. It is a creature of
the ftate, fupported by the ftate, incorporated with the ftate, and governed by a code of laws confirmed by
the ftate---a code, very different from
the facred canons of the New Teftament ; thofe being quite foreign to its
conftitution. Its principal officers are
appointed by the crown ; and, in virtue of ecclefiaftical ftation, are lords
of Parliament*. Nay, even the doc-

D 2

* That our firft Reformers did not approve of
fecular grandeur, power, and employments, being
annexed to the character of bifhops, is very apparent. Thus Mr. TYNDAL, for inftance : " Is it
" not a fhame above all fhames, and a mon-
" ftrous thing, that no man fhould be found able
" to govern a worldly kingdom, fave bifhops and
" prelates, that are taken out of the world,
" and appointed to preach the kingdom of God ?
" To preach God's word is too much for half a
" man : and to minifter a temporal kingdom is
" too much for half a man alfo. Either other
" requireth a whole man - One therefore cannot
" well do both—Wherefore if Chrift's kingdom
" be *not of this world*, nor any of his difciples may
" be otherwife than he was ; then Chrift's vicars,
" which minifter his kingdom in his bodily ab-
" fence. and have the overfight of his flock. may
" be none emperors, kings, dukes, *lords*, knights,

trines profeffed, and the worfhip performed in that eftablifhment, are all
fecularized. Its creeds and forms of
prayer, its numerous rubrics and various rites, are adopted and ufed under
the fanction of civil authority Its Li-.
turgy, therefore, may be juftly confidered as an *Act of Parliament* refpecting,
religious affairs. It muft therefore be
confidered as a kingdom *of this world*.

" temporal judges, or anv other temporal officer ;.
" or, under any falfe names have any fuch domi-
" nion, or minifter any fuch office, as requireth,
" violence." Thus Bp. LATIMER, in his Sermon
" 'of the *Plough :* " This much I dare fay that
" fince *lording* and loitering hath come up, preach-
" ing hath come down, contrary to the Apoftles,
" times For they preached. and *lorded* not :
" and now they *lord* and preach not—Ever fince
" the prelates were made *lords* and nobles, the
" plough ftandeth, there is no work done the
" people ftarve—They are otherwife occupied
" [than in preaching :] fome, in kings matters ;
" fome are ambaffadors : fome, of the privy coun-
" cil : fome, to furnifh the court ; fome, are *lords*
" *of the parliament* ; fome are prefidents, and
" comptrollers of mints. Well, well Is this
" their duty ? Is this their office ? is this their
" calling ? Should we have minifters of the church
" comptrollers of the mints ? Is this a meet of-
" fice for a prieft, that hath cure of fouls ? Is this
" his charge ? I would here afk one queftion I
" would fain know who comtrolleth the devil at
" home in his parifh, while he comtrolleth the.

The tenor of the New Teftament, however, agreeably to our Lord's maxim, leads us to confider particular churches as Congregational ;. and as confilting of thofe who make a credible profeflion of repentance and faith. Such congregations, wherever they be, conftitute the vifible kingdom of Chrift.---That the apoftolic churches were Congregational, is clear from the facred Records ; and that there was no National church for the firft three hundred years, is equally evident. Becaufe there could not be any fuch eftablifhment, till the civil government of fome nation or other profeffed Chriftianity ; which was not the cafe before CONSTANTINE afcended the Imperial throne. Then, indeed, a kind of political Chriftianity came into fafhion, which has continued ever

" mint ? If the apoftles might not leave the of-
" fice of preaching to be deacons fhall we leave it
" for minting ?" Thus Bp Hooper : " Our bi-
" fhops have fo much wit they can rule and
" ferve, as they fay in both ftates : in the church,
" and alfo in the civil policy. When one of
" them is more than any man is able to fatisfy,
" let him do always his beft diligence—They
" know that the primitive church had no fuch
" bifhops as he now a-days " In Mr. PEIRCE's,
Vindicat. of Diffent. Part III. Chap. 1,

since, and is yet in great repute. Nor are National churches likely to fail, while the policy of sovereign princes, and the pride of aspiring prelates can support them. But, being established by human laws, and each of them acknowledging a visible head, either civil or ecclesiastical, either prince or pontiff ; they are secular kingdoms, and unworthy the name of Christian churches.

Once more : As none but regenerate persons belong to the kingdom of Christ, no one is a better subject of his dominion, or a more honorable member of his church, on account of *wealth* or *power*, of *parts* or *learning*. These things, though useful in their places, of much reputation to a secular empire, and of great consequence to it ; neither pertain to the true glory of a Christian church, nor to the sterling worth of a Christian character. For what concern have worldly wealth and civil power, in forming a spiritual character, or in adorning a spiritual kingdom ? The greatest affluence and the highest authority that mortals can enjoy, add nothing to any one's moral worth. No one is a better man, becaufe he is rich and powerful; nor the worfe, becaufe he is poor and in a low ftation. Thefe things are all exterior to moral character. For the moft licentious are often exalted and wealthy, while the moft upright and amiable are loft in obfcurity and oppreffed with want Befides, when wealth, or power, is poffeffed by a true fubject of our Lord's kingdom, the honor attending his character does not arife from his riches, or his authority; but from the holinefs of his life, or his likenefs to Jefus Chrift.

As our Britifh Sovereign is the fountain of honor to all his fubjects, even fo is the King Meffiah to all that are under his dominion. The only way however to be great and honorable in his kingdom, is to be humble, diligent, and ufeful, in promoting the happinefs of our fellow Chriftians and fellow creatures. For among the fundamental laws of Meffiah's empire, the following is one, and it relates to comparative honor : *Whofoever will be great among you, let him be your minifter ; and whofoever will be chief among you, let him be your fervant Even as the Son of man came not to be miniftered unto, but to mi-*

*nifter, and to give his life a ranfom for
many*'This being the law of honor,
and the rule of promotion, in the kingdom of Christ, we may fafely conclude,
that the meaneft domeſtic may be a dignified character in a gofpel church,
and *adorn the doctrine of God our Saviour*:
while his wealthy and powerful maſter,
profeffing the fame faith, may difgrace
the name of a Chriſtian, and bring reproach on the congregation to which
he belongs.   If the former be diligent
and faithful in his menial ſtation : if he
be *found in the faith*, zealous for God,
and heavenly minded ; he is an honorable fubject of Jefus Chriſt, and high
in the eſtimation of Heaven. If, on the
contrary, the latter be formal in his religious profeffion ; if he be unjuft or
haughty, voluptuous or covetous; he
does not belong to the kingdom of
Chriſt, but is manifeſtly a fubject of
Satan.

Nor do the moſt ſhining mental ac-
complifhments, or literary acquifitions,
enter into the true glory of this kingdom. Genius and learning, like wealth
and power, are frequently poffeffed by

---

* Matt. xx. 26, 27. Mark x. 42—45.

the worſt of moral characters. They cannot, therefore, make any part of that excellence by which the ſubjects of Jeſus Chriſt are diſtinguiſhed from thoſe ſecular princes. It is not by the gifts of common Providence, among which parts and learning make a conſpicuous figure ; but by the graces of the Holy Spirit, that any perſon, as a Chriſtian, is worthy of regard.--Yes, it is faith in Chriſt, and obedience to him ; love to God, and benevolence to man ; humility, patience, and reſignation; ſpirituality, and heavenly mindedneſs, which adorn the ſubjects of our Lord's kingdom---which diſtinguiſh them from the children of this world. Theſe, and ſimilar things, reſpect the ſtate of the conſcience, and of the heart. They form a character for eternity, and favour of the heavenly world. Whereas, learning and parts, equally as wealth and power, are quite of a different nature. The diſtinction they make between one another is entirely ſuperficial, and often diſgraced by a profligate heart--belongs only to this world, and has no connection with heaven. But, as will appear in its proper place, the kingdom of Chriſt is nearly allied to heaven--is a ſtate of preparation for

that fublime bleffednefs, an introduction
to its employments, and gives an earneft
of its fruitions. Confequently, the true
glory of that kingdom cannot but con-
lift, in the lively exercife of holy tempers and heavenly affections. The
more there is of a likenefs to heaven, in
the heart and life of any Chriftian; the
more there is of that *honor which comes
from God*, and the more is the caufe of
Chrift adorned.--To be a real fubject of
this kingdom, is a much greater honor
than merely to be a Prophet, or an A-
poftle. For Balaam was the former,
and Judas was the later; yet both of
them were bafe and wretched. *Rejoice
not that the devils are fubject to you; but
rather rejoice that your names are written in heaven. Though I fpeak with the
tongues of men and of angels,--and though
I have the gift of prophecy, and underftand all myfteries and all knowledge; and
though I have all faith, fo that I could re-
move mountains, and have no charity, I am
nothing*, in the eftimate of a fpiritual
Sovereign, or in reference to the heavenly ftate.

No minifter of the word, therefore,
when performing his public work,
fhould ever think of exalting himfelf
as an officer in this kingdom, by dif-

playing his learning, his genius, or his eloquence ; for that would be to *preach himself, not Christ Jesus the Lord* : but, as *in the fight of God*, he should honeſtly aim at *commending himself to every man's conscience, by manifeſtation of the truth.* Then will he imitate a firſt rate miniſter in the Meſſiah's kingdom, and obtain the approbation of his divine Sovereign.--Beſides, in the diſplays of profound learning, by critical diſquiſitions; of great acumen, by metaphyſical ſpeculations ; or of a ſparkling genius, by agreeable turns of wit. Chriſt and conſcience feel their intereſts but little concerned. The former is too obſervant of the preacher's motives, and too jealous of his own honor, to be pleaſed with ſuch a procedure ; and the latter is either too ſleepy to be arouſed, or too much pained to receive relief, by thoſe means. If our Lord conſider himſelf as honored by the preacher's labours, and if the miniſter have any reaſon to expect ſucceſs, it muſt be by a faithful and ſimple promulgation of revealed truths----thoſe truths which regard ſupreme authority in the divine law, and ſaving grace in the glorious goſpel--thoſe truths, I will add, which

E

lie open to common capacities. If the conscience receive advantage, it is by the operation of the same truths; either as convincing of sin and enforcing duty, or as revealing pardon and affording peace. But the honor of Christ and the tranquility of conscience are seldom promoted, in a public ministry, by the researches of learning, or the refinements of genius: for they are too sacred, and too spiritual, to acknowledge their obligations to such things.

The kingdom of Christ is not of this world, with regard to the means he employed in its first establishment, and those he appointed for its enlargement and support. Craft and violence, injustice and cruelty, have been commonly used in the founding, supporting, and extending of secular kingdoms. The Roman empire was founded, and grew to its height, in blood. Even the Jewish republic was established, enlarged, and defended by force of arms. The Canaanitish nations, on account of their enormous wickedness, were exterminated by the sword of Israel; or, if spared by the chosen tribes, became tributary to them. This, though ac-

cording to Jehovah's appointment, as
the great Proprietor of the whole earth;
and though a righteous execution of
punishment, for acts of rebellion
against the Eternal Sovereign; was a
plain indication that, in various respects, the Israelitish church was a
kingdom of this world. Such also was
that kingdom of the Messiah which the
carnal Jews in our Lord's time vainly
expected, whenever the great promise
made to their fathers should be fulfilled:
for they dreamed of being exalted to
the highest pitch of political grandeur,
and of having all the other nations under their control.---The principle
instruments employed by princes, to
establish, maintain, and extend their dominions, are--not persons the most remarkable for integrity and benevolence, for piety and philanthropy; but
those who are most eminent for political prudence, or martial bravery; for
secret intrigue, or open hostility--
those who are best qualified to persuade by eloquence, to circumvent by
cunning, or to subdue by force.

But the most illustrious instruments
employed by our Anointed Prince in the
erecting of his monarchy, were of a

character quite the reverſe. They
were chiefly ſelected from the lower
orders of life, and called from occupa-
tions eſteemed mean. Uneducated in
the courts of royalty, in the ſchools of
learning, or in the field of war; they
were ſtrangers to the fineſſe of politici-
ans, little acquainted with Gentile phi-
loſophy, and unpractiſed in the art of
eloquence. It may be juſtly preſum-
ed, therefore, that a ſtrong degree of
ruſticity appeared in their dreſs, their
aſpect, and their accent: for they were
apparently *unlearned and unpoliſhed men*.
So ignorant were they of ſciences called liberal, ſo unpolite in their addreſs,
and ſo uncanonical in their garb, that
multitudes called Chriſtians, it is highly
probable, would be aſhamed to give
them a hearing, were they now preſent
among us ; unleſs the public attention
were firſt excited, by the exerciſe of
their miraculous powers.--Yes, by the
inſtrumentality of thoſe unlettered and
plain men did our Lord erect his kingdom, or eſtabliſh the goſpel church.
In making war upon Satan's empire,
evangelical truth and ſpiritual gifts,
laborious preaching and ardent prayer,
fortitude, patience, and a holy example, were the arms they uſed. Such

were the militia, and such the armour, employed by our divine Sovereign; yet perfectly suited to the nature of his kingdom. For it is an empire, not of secular power and external pomp; but of truth and of righteousness, of love and of peace.

Were the Messiah's kingdom *of this world*, his loyal subjects might lawfully take the sword, to repel assailants and subdue his enemies: for without the liberty of such defence, no secular state can long subsist. This, however, he absolutely pohibited : which prohibition is founded in the peculiar nature of his kingdom. For thus he speaks, to one who thought of defending his person and cause by force ; *Put up thy sword into the sheath.* Soon after, on another occasion, he said ; *If my kingdom were of this world, then would my servants fight, that I should not be delivered to the Jews : but now is my kingdom not from hence*[*]. As by the particle *now*, our spiritual Sovereign apparently refers to his kingdom among the Jews ; so he seems to distinguish his dominion in the gospel church, from that over the Israelitish nation. E 2

* Joh. xviii. 11, 36.

In former times, the Holy Spirit frequently came upon the subjects of Jehovah's government, to inspire them with martial courage for the defence of his kingdom, and to destroy his enemies. Hence, among the ancient worthies, we read of those who *subdued kingdoms, waxed valiant in fight, and put to flight the armies of the aliens.* But the disciples of Christ being called to a different kind of conflict, divine energy is granted for a different purpose. The military service of a Christian, as such, is entirely of a spiritual nature. It is a *good fight of faith :* a *striving against sin,* in himself, and in the world around him : a *holding fast the profession of his faith,* in spite of all opposition. The Christian hero is conformed to the captain of salvation, in maintaining the truth, and in bearing the cross ; in enduring the contradiction of sinners, and in despising the shame that is cast upon him. His accoutrements are, as Paul informs us, *The girdle of truth,* and *the breastplate of righteousness ; the shield of faith, and helmet of hope,* and *the sword of the Spirit**. Such is the armour provided by the King Messiah for his devoted

* Ephef. vi. 10—18. 1 Theff. v. 8. 2 Cor. x. 3, 4 5.

subjects; by which they are enabled
to defend themselves, and to promote
the general interests of his kingdom.
This holy empire depends not upon
power, wealth, or learning, either for
ornament or support. *Not by might,
nor by power, but by my Spirit, saith Jehovah.*

Neither the force of *secular power,*
nor the arts of *carnal policy,* ought therefore to be used in promoting the cause
of Christ : such things being quite abhorrent from his intention, and from
the nature of his kingdom. The great
design of our Lord in founding a Spiritual empire was, to display the perfections of God in the holiness and happiness of his chosen people. The kingdom of Christ, as before observed, is a
dominion of truth and of rectitude, of
love and of peace. Now the interests
of such a monarchy, and the end pro-
posed by it, cannot be promoted by any
other than spiritual means, and those
of divine appointment. It is only so
far as the minds of men are enlightened
by heavenly truth, their consciences
impressed with God's authority, and
their hearts engaged on spiritual things,
that the cause of Christ is advanced.

But in what way shall persecuting force
be applied, to irradiate the dark understanding, to arouse the stupid conscience, and to sanctify the depraved heart?
It is only by the fruits of an adoring affection for God, of sincere love to the
brethren, and of cordial goodwill to all
mankind, that our Lord is honored, or
his end answered, by the subjects of his .
dominion. How, then, shall coercive
measures increase those fruits of holi- .
ness ? Or how, shall malevolence, in
any of its infernal forms, be employed
to support a kingdom of love and of ‹
peace.

Nor are the contrivances of carnal ›
policy less foreign to the nature of this
kingdom, than the exertions of secular
power. For what has the policy of
princes, or of prelates, to do in maintaining; or in extending, an empire of
truth and of rectitude ? Truth seeks no
subterfuge, and rectitude fears no exa-
mination: but the operations of policy
are subtle, and its first designs are latent.
The policy of great men may form ci- .
vil establishments of Christianity, and
adorn the exterior of public worship.
It may dignify ministers of the word
with pompous titles, unknown to the ‹

New Teſtament, and inveſt them with temporal power, till their claim of ſucceeding to the Apoſtles becomes an inſult upon common ſenſe. Theſe and ſimilar things may be effected by it, under the fair pretext of rendering religion reſpectable, and of making it more general : but the empire of Jeſus Chriſt diſdains them all, becauſe they belong to the kingdoms of this world.

But though our Lord neither needs, nor accepts, the puny arts of men, to advance his cauſe and ſupport his intereſts ; yet various methods have been deviſed by accleſiaſtics, to obviate *the offence of the croſs*, to render themſelves reſpectable, and to promote ſomething called *Chriſtianity*. That they might not be thought, like the Fiſhermen of Galilee, *unlearned and ignorant* perſons, they have eagerly ſought literary titles, and to be called *Rabbi*. To adorn the miniſterial office, and to ſanction their adminiſtrations, they have been as careful as Jewiſh prieſts to appear in canonicals. To prevent the pride of their hearers being diſguſted, certain humiliating truths have been kept out of ſight ; and that the conſciences of others might not be pained, ſoftening in-

terpretations of divine precepts have
been given. To stand free from a suf-
picion of bigotry, the importance of
capital truths has been surrendered;
and to keep fair with something called
charity, it has been agreed that human
inventions should hold the place of divine institutions.--Many of the clerical
character, in our National Establishment, have deliberately subscribed
what they did not believe ; solemnly
professed their consent to what they
could not approve ; and frequently
practised, as part of their public devo-
tions, what they were constrained to
wish had never existed*. Nay, as if
the ministers of that Establishment pof-
fessed a righteous monopoly of publish-
ing evangelical truth, and of admini-
stering divine institutions, numbers of
them have sworn to persecute their
Protestant Diffenting neighbours, for
daring to hold separate assemblies†.

* For can any man upon earth really believe
all that is contained in the *Thirty Nine Articles*,
and cordially approve of *every thing* contained in
the *Book of Common Prayer* ?
† Thus runs part of an Oath which is taken by
Graduates in the University of Oxford Item fpe-
cialiter tu jurabis, quod intenullas communitates,
vel perfonas iftius Univerfitatis, impedies pacem,
concordiam et amorem—*Nec Conventiculis intereffe*

Thus multitudes have subscribed and consented, trimed and sworn, to promote the interests of a spiritual kingdom--a kingdom of truth, of love, and of peace !

debes. nec eis tacite vel expreff: confentire ; SED EA POTIUS, MODIS QUIBUS POTERIS IMPEDIRE. *Ex-cerp. e Corp. Statut. Univerfit. Oxon.* Tit. IX. Sect. vi. § 1. That is, *You shall in a particular manner swear, that you will not obftruct peace, harmony and love, among any communities, or perfons, of this Uni-verfity—Nor ought you to be prefent in Conventicles, nor either expreßly nor tacitly confent to them* BUT RATHER HINDER THEM BY ANY MEANS IN YOUR POWER.—How any man, at all acquainted with the rights of confcience, can take this Oath ; or, having taken it, can treat Diffenters as Chriftian brethren, without renouncing his own Conformity, I cannot imagine. A more fhocking dilemma can fcarcely be conceived : for it is *perfecution* on the one hand, and *perjury* on the other.—Of a fimilar complexion is the eleventh Canon of the Church of England, which is entitled, *Maintainers of Conventicles cenfured,* and it reads thus : " Whofoever fhall hereafter affirm or maintain, " That there are within this realm other meet- " ings, affemblies, or congregations of the king's " born fubjects, than fuch as by the laws of this " land are held and allowed, which may rightly " challenge to themfelves the name of true and " lawful churches : Let him be excommunicated, " and not reftored, but by the archbifhop, after " his repentance, and public revocation of fuch " his wicked errors."—I will here fubjoin the following remark of Dr. OWEN : " There is in

Some, of different communions, have deliberately acted as if the preacher's work were a mere trial of skill, and as if a pulpit were the stage of a harlequin. To display the fertility of their invention, they have selected for texts mere scraps of scripture language; which, so far from containing complete propositions, have not, in their dislocated state conveyed a single idea. Upon these they have harangued; while the ignorant multitude have been greatly surprised that the preacher could find so much, where common capacities perceived nothing.--Sometimes these men

---

" this [ecclesiastical] Conformity required a re-
" nunciation of all other ways of public worship,
" or means of edification, that may be made use
" of. For they are all expressly forbidden in the
" rule of the Conformity. No man, therefore, can
" comply with that rule but that a renunciation
" of all other public ways of edification as *un-
" lawful* is part of the visible profession which
" they make. *Video meliora proboque, deteriora,*
" *sequor.* is no good plea in religion. It is up-
" rightness and integrity that will preserve men,
" and nothing else. He that shall endeavor to
" cheat his conscience by distinctions, and mental
" reservations, in any concernments of religious
" worship, I fear he hath little of it, if any at all,
" that is good for aught." *Enquiry into the Orig.
Nature, Institut. and Commun. of Evang. Churches,*
p. 228, 229.

of genius will choofe paffages of Scripture expreffive of plain hiftorical facts,
which have no connection with the
great work of falvation by Jefus Chrift;
and handle them (not profeffedly by
way of accommodation, for then it
might be admitted) but as if they were
facred allegories. Such hiftorical facts-
being *fpiritualized,* as they love to call
it, doctrines, privileges, duties, in
abundance, are eafily derived from
them. Nay, fo ingenious are preachers
of this turn, that it is no hard matter
for them to find a great part of their
creed in almoft any text they take.
Thus they allegorize common fenfe
into pious abfurdity.--It might, perhaps, be too barefaced, though it would
certainly fuit the vanity of fuch preachers, were they frequently to addrefs
their hearers on the pronominal mo-
nofyllable *I* : and there are two paffages of facred Writ where it occurs in
the moft appofite manner. The former
would make an admirable text ; the
latter, a noble conclufion : and they
are as follows : " Such a man as *I*--Is
" not this great Babylon that *I* have

built* ? Others, and often the same
persons, frequently use the gestures of
the theatre, and the language of a
mountebank : as if their business were
to amuse, to entertain, and to make their
hearers laugh. Extravagant attitudes
and quaint expressions, idle stories and
similies quite ludicrous, appear in abundance, and constitute no small part of
the entertainment furnished by such
characters. But in what a state must
the consciences of those preachers be,
who can deliberately and with preme-

---

* Mr. G GREGORY, when animadverting on
the conduct which is here censured, says ; " It is
" dangerous on any occasion to depart from the
" plain track of common sense : and there is no
" attempt at ingenuity so easy as that which bor-
" ders upon nonsense—It is one of the mean arti-
" fices of barren genius, to surprise the audience
" with a text consisting of one or two words. I
" have heard of a person of this description, who
" preached from *Jehovah Jireh* , and another,
" from the monosyllable, *But* These are con-
" temptible devices, more adapted to the moving
" theatre of the mountebank than to the pulpit, and
" can only serve to captivate the meanest and most
" ignorant of the vulgar." *Sermons*, Introduct. p.
14, 15, 18 —Mr. CLAUDE says, " Never choose
" such texts as have not a complete sense ; for on-
" ly impertinent and foolish people will attempt to
" preach from one or two words, which signify
" nothing." *Essay on Composit. of a Serm.* Vol. I.
p. 3.

ditation act in this manner! Or, what muft we think of their petitions for divine affiltance, in addrefling the people, when they intend thus to treat them!--I called it *entertainment*; and, furely, they themfelves do not confider it in a religious point of light. For can any man, who is not infane deliberately adopt meafures of this kind, when really aiming, either to produce, or to promote, a devotional and heavenly temper in the hearts of his hearers? Yet that is the general end of preaching. Or can the preacher have any devotion, while fhowing the airs of a mountebank; and when, if the bulk of his auditory had no more decency than himfelf, there would be a burft of laughter throughout the affembly? Whatever fuch declaimers may think, where there is no folemnity, there is no devotion: and, we may venture to add, that a perfon habitually deftitute of devotion in his own heart, while pretending to teach others the doctrine of Chrift, is a wretched character in the fight of God, and has reafon to tremble. Such a man ferves not our Lord Jefus Chrift, but his own interefts, in fome form or other. He may wifh for popularity, and perhaps may obtain it from the ignorant multitude; but people of fenfe and of piety will confider him as difgracing his office, as affronting their underftandings, and as infulting the majefty of that Divine Pre- fence in which he ftands. For where, upon earth, are we to expect folemnity, if not in the pulpit? There, a man fhould be ferious and folemn as death.

It may perhads be faid; "This kind "of trifling has its ufe. It is a mean "of exciting curiofity, and of draw- "ing many to hear the gofpel, who "might not otherwife have the leaft "inclination fo to do." Such, I pre- fume, is the chief reafon by which preachers of this caft endeavour to juf- tify themfelves at the bar of their own confciences. In anfwer to which, a re- petition of that capital faying, *My king- dom is not of this world*, might be fuffici- ent : for that muft be a wretched caufe, even of a fecular kind, which needs buffoonery to fupport it. To trifle in the fervice of God, is to be profane. It is, therefore, an impious kind of tri- fling : and *fhall we do evil that good may come* ?--Through the interference of Providence, and the fovereign grace of God, various inftances of enormous wickedneſs have iſſued in the higheſt good to mankind. Of this we have undoubted evidence in the ſelling of Joſeph by his envious brethren. We have a ſtill more ſtriking inſtance in the death of Chriſt, through the treachery of Judas and malice of the Jews. Nay, perſecution has *frequently* been an occaſion of ſpreading the goſpel : yet few, I take it for granted, have perſecuted for that end, or attempted to juſtify the practice upon that principle. Were the farcical conduct, here cenſured, lawful, there would be reaſon to think that the cauſe of Chriſt, and the intereſts of harlequin, are very nearly allied ; becauſe the ſame kind of means is adapted to promote them.

The Seraphim, however, in Iſaiah's viſion, and the Apoſtles of Chriſt, appear to have had a very different view of the caſe. The *former* (who ſeem to be an emblem of apoſtolic miniſters*,) are preſented to notice, as performing the ſervice of their Sublime Sovereign with profoundeſt awe. Struck with the majeſty of his appearance, and penetrated by the authority of his commands,

F 2

* Vid. *Vitringam in loc.*

they adore and obey with all humility, and with all folemnity. Agreeably to which, the *latter* give it as divine law,. that thofe who would perform accepta- ble worfhip, muft do it *with reverence; and godly fear.* This law of devotion,. they further inform us, is founded in the; nature of things ; as appears by the reafon affigned to enforce the precept, *For our God is* A CONSUMING FIRE. Such is the Chriftian's God, with regard to his purity, his jealoufy, and his juftice*.

Conformable to this idea of that Su- blime Being whom every preacher pro- feffes to ferve, was the conduct of Paul when difpenfing the gofpel. For, in oppofition to fome who *handled the word of God deceitfully,* to amufe the carnal and win their affections ; he la- boured, *by manifeftation of the truth,* to *commend himfelf to every man's confci- ence, as in the fight of God.* Truth, con- fcience, and God ! What facred and folemn ideas! Yet Paul, as a preacher, habitually acted under their influence. That evangelical truth might be difplay ed, that the human confcience might be impreffed, and that the will of God

* Heb. xii. 28, 29. Deut. iv. 24. ix. 3.

might be performed, were all included in his defign How foreign are thefe particulars from every thing of a farci- cal nature! Nor can any perfon who confiders himfelf, when preaching the word, as having eternal truth for the fubject of his difcourfe, the confcien- ces of men for the objects of his regard, and the omnicient God for a witnefs of his conduct, be otherwife than folemn: for fuch an one will fpeak, as knowing that he *muft give an account.*--When hearing a minifter who acts in charac- ter, and copics the example of Paul, we are led to reflect on that ancient oracle; *I will be fanctified in them that come nigh me*, to perform facred fervice. But when fitting under the effufions of a pul- pit buffoon, the language of an Egypti- an tyrant occurs to remembrance; *Who is Jehovah, that I fhould obey him?* or what is his worfhip, that I fhould treat it with reyerence?

When a fermon was expected from Peter, by Cornelius and his friends, the centurion exprefled himfelt thus: *We are all here prefent before God, to hear all things that are commanded thee of God.* Thefe Gentiles, it is manifeft, were pe- netrated with devout folemnity, and

filled with holy expectation. Not being affembled for carnal amufement,
but in order to know and perform the
will of God ; they confidered themfelves as in the Divine Prefence: and
fo did their infpired teacher. A worthy example for us to follow, when
convened to preach and to hear the
word of truth. But how contrary to
this is that pulpit drollery, which is the
object of our cenfure ! For it converts
the folemn fervice of God (fhocking
metamorphofis!) into carnal amufement, upon which numbers indeed attend with pleafure, but with no more
devotion than if they were in a play-
houfe.

Is there any raefon to be furprifed
that men of fenfe, who are already pre-
judiced againft the genuine gofpel,
fhould have their difaffection to evangelical truths increafed, when they find
thofe truths avowed, and their importance loudly urged, by merryandrews?
If, inftead of *found fpeech, which cannot
be condemned*, they meet with extrava-
gance and nonfenfe, what will thy fay?
Is there any reafon to wonder, that In-
fidels fhould thence take occafion to re-
dicule the Scripture, as calculated to

ferve the meaneft purpofes ; or that they fhould contemptuoufly call preaching *prieftcraft?* If thofe who profefs to love revealed truths drefs them up in a fool's coat, for the entertainment of their hearers, will Deifts forbear to laugh? If, where the *man of God* fhould be heard, with all folemnity warning finners *to flee from the wrath to come,* and intreating them *to be reconciled to God*; a farcical droll appear, fpouting low wit and provoking refibility, will the Infidel fay ; " The " preacher himfelf does not believe " the Chriftian miniftry to be a divine " appointment, nor the exercife of it " a devotional fervice; but he finds it " convenient for fecular purpofes to " make pretences of that kind?--Among all the devices of carnal policy for the fupport and enlargement of our Lord's kingdom, there are none more contemptible, and few more deteftable, than of converting the pulpit into a ftage of entertainment. Of this mind was an old Nonconformift minifter, when he faid ; " Of all preaching in " the world I hate that moft, which " has a tendency to make the hearers " laugh ; or to affect their minds with " fuch levity. as ftage-plays do, inftead

" of affecting them with an holy reve-
" rence for the name of God. We
" should suppose, as it were, when we
" draw near him in holy things, that
" we saw the throne of God, and the
" millions of glorious angels attend-
" ing him ; that we may be awed with
" his majesty, lest we profane his ser-
" vice, and take his name in vain."---
To the pulpit harlequin we may therefore apply the following lines ;

" If angels tremble, 'tis at such a sight :
" More struck with grief, or wonder, who can tell?" ·

*The kingdom of Christ is not of this
world, in regard to the laws by which it is
governed.* Secular kingdoms are under
the direction of human laws, which are
frequently weak, partial, and unjust---
of laws which, when least imperfect,
extend their obliging power no further
than the exterior behaviour : for it
would be vain and foolish in a temporal sovereign, to think of giving law to
the thoughts, or desires, of any subject.
Civil penalties are the sanction of human laws, and external force gives them
their energy.--Not so the laws of this
holy empire. For, proceeding from
Him, in whom are *are all the treasures
of knowledge,* they must be consumately

'wife: being enacted by Him who is inflexibly just and supremely kind, they cannot but be perfectly good : being given by him who searches the heart and is Lord of conscience, their obligation extends to the latent desire, and the rising conception. Controuling the thoughts and binding the conscience, their sanction is entirely spiritual The motives enforcing obedience to them, are the smiles, or the frowns, of Him who has our everlasting all at his disposal.

As is the kingdom, such is the sovereign ; and as the sovereign, such are his laws. If the kingdom be *of this world*, it must have a political sovereign ; whose laws must be coercive, and confined to exterior behaviour. But if the kingdom be of a spiritual kind, the sovereign must be so too. His laws must extend no less to the conscience, than to the conversation, and be enforced by sanctions of a spiritual nature. Such is the King Messiah, and such are the laws of his kingdom.

The subjects of our divine Sovereign may be considered, either as detatched individuals, or as united in distinct so-

cieties, and vifibly profeffing their fubjection to his authority. Hence the
execution of thofe laws by which they
are governed, comes under a twofold
confideration. *As detatched individuals,*
the application of his laws to particular cafes, is entirely with him, and
with the confcience of each individual.
As united in diftinct focieties, which are
called particular churches, his laws of
admiffion, of worfhip, and of exclufion,
are to be applied by the community--
applied, not under the influence of carnal motives, but under the operation of
his authority, and for purpofes entirely
fpiritual.

By the laws of this kingdom, a credible profeffion of repentance and faith
is required of all, previous to baptifm.
Such profeffion being confidered as an
evidence of their *fellowfhip in the gofpel,*
and of willing fubjection to the authority of Chrift, they are entitled to memberfhip in a particular church. On
this ground they are admitted : nor do
they forfeit their memberfhip, except
by fome capital departure from *that*
gofpel, or fome flagrant offence againft
this authority.--But as, by the laws of
our heavenly Sovereign, their admiffion

to vifible fellowſhip was entirely for
ſpiritual purpoſes, their excluſion from
it does not include temporal diſadvan-
tages   Their ſituation as men, and as
the ſubjects of a political ſtate, not being altered by their church-relation
commencing ; they ſhould not be af-
fected, in thoſe reſpects, by the diſſo-
lution of that relation. For as the
laws of Chriſt ſay nothing about the ad-
miſſion of one or another, on account
of his domeſtic or civil connections ;
nor yet for his wealth or influence, his
parts or learning ; ſo they are equally
ſilent about pecuniary fines and ſatisfac-
tory penances, about civil diſabilities
and corporal puniſhments, attending
the excluſion of any offender. The
former being quite foreign to qualifications for a ſpiritual kingdom, the latter muſt be utterly abhorrent from the
laws by which it is governed ; being
manifeſtly the inventions of Antichriſt,
and the ſupporters of his cruel throne.
Civil penalties, in this caſe, are adapted
to generate fear, and promote hypo-
criſy ; to ſuppreſs truth, and render
Chriſtianity itſelf ſuſpicious.

Here we perceive another disparity between the Jewish and the Christian church. For under the Old Oecono- my, the laws of religion were sanctified by *temporal politics*, and frequently those of the severest kind*. To be cast out of the congregation, to be forbid- den access to the sanctuary worship, (except for ceremonial pollution) was to be deprived, not only of ecclesiasti- cal privileges, but also of civil rights. The church and the state being coex- tended, and including the same persons, an exclusion from the former was an expulsion from the latter; whether it was by a sentence of capital punish- ment, or in some other way. But this, like many other things, was peculiar to that Dispensation. It was founded in the National form of their church- state, and in their Theocracy. Thence it was that blasphemy and idolatry were punished with death, as being high- treason against their divine Sovereign. That Oeconomy being abolished, the church of God has taken a new form. *The priesthood being changed, there is of*

---

* See Exod. xii. 53, 19. xxx. 33, 38. xxxi. 14. Lev. vii. 20—27. xvii. 3—9. xix. 8. xxiii. 27, 28, 29. Numb. ix. 13. xv. 30, 31. xix. 13. with ma- ny other similar places.

neceffity a change alfo of the law, relating to the conftitution, members, and government of the church. The laws of admiffion, and of exclufion, muft therefore be very different; as well as thofe pertaining to public worfhip. Now, to underftand thefe laws, we muft ftudy --not the Pentateuch of Mofes; much lefs the *Provinciale* of LYNDWOOD, or the *Codex* of GIBSON, but---the New Teftament of Jefus Chrift. To reafon from the conftitution and form, the laws and government, the privileges and rites of the Jewifh, to thofe of the chriftian church; is to adopt a capital principle of Papal depravity, and grofsly to corrupt our holy religion.

Our divine Sovereign has alfo provided for the edification of his loyal fubjects, by ordinances and rites of 'worfhip, no lefs than for the government of his kingdom. As King of the Chriftian church, it conftitutes a diftinguifhed part of his royal prerogative, to prefcribe the whole of that fpiritual fervice which is to be performed. Of this prerogative Jehovah was always jealous: nor, under the former Oeconomy, did he ever more inftantly, or more feverely punifh, than when his

orders about the affairs of religion were
difregarded; even though, as in the
cafe of Uzzah, the motive appeared
laudable.--What is religion, in its various branches, but that obedience
which is due to God? And what is obedience, but fubmiffion to his authority?
Now, as authority exerts itfelf in commands, there cannot be obedience, there
cannot be holy worfhip, where there
is no divine command, either explicit
or implicit. *Who hath required this at
your hands?* *In vain do ye worfhip me,
teaching for doctrines the commandments
of men*--exclude and condemn a great
number of things, which millions
efteem ornamental and ufeful in the
worfhip of God.

Strange, that any Proteftant church
fhould avowedly claim a " power to
" decree rites or ceremonies" in the
folemn fervice of our divine Lord!
As if he were not the legiflator in
his own kingdom! Or as if, though
poffeffed of authority, he had not wifdom enough to provide for his own
honor; or were defective in goodnefs,
refpecting his faithful fubjects! But
whatever the compilers and the fub-
fcribers of a National Creed may

think, to perform rites which Chrift did not appoint, and to alter thofe which he enjoined, are vile impeach-ments of his royal character, and mult expofe to his refentment. The former ufurps his throne : the latter annuls his laws.--*Strange*, did I fay? the ex-preffion mult be recalled. For there is no reafon to wonder that a National reli-gious eftablifhment, with a political fo-vereign for its head, fhould make the claim I have jult mentioned. Who can doubt whether the fame authority which conftitutes, governs, and fupports a community for any particular purpofe, may not prefcribe to that community with a view to the end intended by it? But things fhould not be called by wrong names; and to denominate fuch an efta-blifhment *a church of Chrift*, is a grofs mifnomer.

The kingdom of Chrift is not like the em-pires of this world, in regard to external fplendor. The grandeur of a temporal kingdom chiefly confifts, in the number and affluence of its nobility, the titles and pompous appearance of its various magiftrates, the flourifhing flate of its trade and commerce, the wealth of its

yeomanry, and the elegance of its public buildings. Magnificent palaces and
royal robes are quite in character for
secular princes. Enfigns of honor,
fplendid equipages, and ftately manfions, are fuitable to the nobles : while
a more folemn kind of exterior pomp is
very becoming the minifters of public
juftice. Thefe and fimilar things give
an air of dignity, and of importance,
to political fovereignties : but they are
all foreign to the kingdom of Chrift, the
glory of which is entirely fpiritual --
The Chriftian Church is dignified and
adorned, by being the depofitary of divine truth in its unadulterated ftate, and
by practifing divine appointments in
their primitive purity ; by poffefling
the beauties of holinefs, and by enjoy-
ing the prefence of God. Such is the
true glory of our Lord's kingdom,
which renders it incomparably fuperior
to every temporal monarchy.

It muft therefore be very abfurd to
think of doing honor to Chriftianity, by
erecting *pompous places* of worfhip, by
confecrating thofe places, and by adorning with *jhowy veftments*, in the performance of public worfhip. Let the
palaces of princes, and the manfions of

the mighty, be magnificent and richly ornamented ;. let the nobles and judges of the land, when acting agreeably to their different characters, appear in robes of state and in robes of magistracy; as those things belong to the kingdoms *of this world*, nor pretend to any thing more, there is nothing amiss, nothing inconsistent with station or profession. But confine them there, and by no means think of decorating the kingdom, or of promoting the cause of Christ, by any thing similar. Were any man to lacker gold, and paint the diamond, to increase their lustre, he would certainly be considered as insane Yet the conduct of those persons is more absurd, who borrow the trappings of secular kingdoms, to adorn the spiritual kingdom of Jesus Christ.

As to *places of worship*, conveniency is all that is wanted, and all that becomes the simplicity of Christianity. To. lay the first stone of such an edifice with solemn formalities, is Jewish* : to dedicate it, when completed, to any particular faint, is manifestly superstitious : to consecrate it by any solemn form, looks as if it succeeded to the honors of.

---

*.Ezra iii. 10. 11.

Solomon's temple; as if the Deity were expected to reside in it, rather than grant his presence to the congregation worshipping there; and as if it were to possess a relative holiness, like that of the ancient sanctuary. I may venture to add, that any religious parade at the first opening of such a place, is apparently inconsistent with the idea of all distinction of places, in regard to worship, being abolished, and too much resembles a Jewish, or a Popish consecration*.

---

* I will here subjoin a few particulars mentioned by Mr. *James Owen*, relative to Consecrations. He shows, that the Israelites dedicated not only the tabernacle and temple, but also their private houses, and their cities (Deut. xx. 5. Psalm xxx. *title*. Nehem. xii. 27.)---That the Jewish synagogues were not consecrated, nor esteemed holy, as the temple was---That the consecration of places for Christian worship was invented in the time of *Constantine*---That Christians had not long been in possession of consecrated temples, before they thought it expedient to furnish them with altars; and being provided with altars, they afterwards invented the sacrifice of the mass---That the Papists, like the old Pagan Romans, first consecrate the ground, and then the edifice erected upon it---That *Durandus* argues for the consecration of churches, from the example of Nebuchadnezzar dedicating his golden image---That Roman Catholics consecrate, with various and solemn formalities, the first foundation stone of a building intended for public worship---That they consecrate bells, priests-garments, and almost every thing belonging to their corrupted

In regard to *ministers*, when attending to any branch of their holy function, let them not think of heightening their own importance, or of promoting the cause of Christ, by imitating Jewish or pagan priests, adorned with peculiar habits, when performing their different rites. If Christian ministers be decently clothed, when in their own families, when visiting their friends, or when walking the streets; why should they not be considered as properly habited for the performance of their sacred office? What reason can be assigned for the use of any particular dress, when engaged in public service, that would not militate against the spirituality of our Lord's kingdom, and the simplicity of his worship?

worship---That though in England, since the Reformation. it does not appear that any Form for the consecrating of churches, and of burying grounds, has received the sanction of public authority; yet various Forms for those purposes have been published and used---That the consecrating bishop *blesses* the church or chapel, and prays " that " that the blessed Spirit would send down on the " place, *his sanctifying power and grace*"---That he consecrates the font, the pulpit, the reading-desk, the communion table, the paten, the chalice, and so on. *Hist. of Conscerat. of Altars, Temples, and Churches,* passim.

It may, perhaps, be said ; "Clerical
" habits are indifferent and harmlefs
" things, except when they are impo-
" fed." But if fo, the idea of impofi-
tion being excluded, the canonical drefs
of a Popifh prieft, the red hat of a car-
dinal, and the triple crown of a pontiff,
may all be juftified : for, in themfelves,
they are equally harmlefs as the gown,
the furplice, or the band. Innocent,
however, as all thefe peculiarities are,
detached from the minifterial character, and from holy worfhip ; the *reafon*
or *motive* of wearing them in facred
fervice, may be carnal, bafe, and finful.
In fome, there is too much ground of
fufpicion, a defire of being efteemed
by the vulgar, either as perfons of
learning, or as epifcopally ordained,
when they are not fo ; and, in others,
a luft of increafing their learned and
prieftly importance, are the latent rea-
fons of wearing thofe idle badges of
clerical diftinction. But when illiterate men affume the garb of learning,
their vanity is contemptible : when
they intend, by fo doing, to obtain that
refpect from the ignorant, of which
they know themfelves unworthy, their
practical falfehood is deteftable : and
when any minifter thinks of magnify-.

ing his office, by pompofity in the pulpit, he betrays his ignorance relating to
the nature of that kingdom in which he
profeffes to be an officer.--Do the laws
of this holy empire forbid the fubjects
to affect fhining and coftly apparel, as
not becoming thofe who *profefs godli-
nefs** ; and will not the principle of
that prohibition apply with increafing
force to the cafe before us? Is it in-
confiftent with that fpiritual mindednefs, of which every avowed difciple
of Chrift makes an implicit profeffion,
to be fond of a fhowy drefs in the intercourfes of common life; and can it be
fuitable to the fimplicity of Chriftian
worfhip, to the character of its Lord,
or to the example of his Apoftles, for
minifters to make a more grand appearance, and take more ftate upon them,
when performing their folemn fervice,
than at any other time? Let thefe who
underftand the Chriftian fyftem, and are
heavenly minded, form the determina-
tion.

It muft indeed be acknowledged, that
the ancient people of God had a fplendid fanctuary, and a fumptuous temple;

---

* 1 Tim. ii. 9, 10, 1 Pet. iii. 3, 4.

that the Jewish priests, when performing sacred service, apeared in holy gar-
ments ; and that the highpriest, on certain occasions, was richly adorned, in
a manner peculiar to his office. But
then it is plain, that those things were
expressly appointed by Jehovah ; that
the Dispensation to which they belonged was of a typical nature ; that they
were suited to the church while in a state
of minority ; that the whole Jewish
nation was then the visible church ; that
Jehovah was not only the God, but also
the King of that nation ; that the ancient sanctuary was a palace, where political royalty resided*, as well as a temple, where Deity was adored ; and
that the priests were officers in the state,
as well as ministers of religion. To
such a politico-ecclesiastical kingdom
the splendor of the sanctuary, and the
dress of the priests, were manifestly
adapted. Hence the tabernacle is called *a worldly sanctuary*, and the rites
performed there *elements of the world*†.
To these, the heavenly sanctuary, into
which our Great High priest is entered,
and the spiritual worship of the Christian church, stand opposed.--It should

* Matt. v. 35. † Heb. ix 1. Gal. 4?, 9. Col. ii.
8, 20.

not be forgotten, that though the Son
of God, when difplaying his glory as
King of the Jewifh ftate, took up his
abode in the fanctuary, as in a royal palace ; yet, when *he came into his own
country**, as King of the Gofpel Church,
he had not *where to lay his head*.

What, then, have the fplendor, the
laws, or the rites of Judaifm, to do in
the New Oeconomy ; except we mean
to convert the Chriftian church into the
Jewifh temple ? Grandeur and fhow,
whether as pertaining to places of worfhip, or to minifters of the word, are
abhorrent from the Gofpel Difpenfation : nor, under the prefent Oeconomy,
have they any other tendency, than to
gratify that pride from which they ori-
ginate, and to give the kingdom of
Chrift a fecular appearance.--The New
Oeconomy being intended for all nations and all fucceeding ages, is equally
fitted for the rich and the poor : nor
does it make any diftinction, in regard
to places, where its worfhip fhould be
performed. That God be adored *in
fpirit and in truth*, according to his own
rule, is all it requires of one congrega-

H

* Joh. i. 11. See Dr. *Doddridge* in loc.

tion or of another. It difdains, therefore, to borrow any part of its glory,
from the grandeur of an edifice, or from
the garb of a minister. Though far
from fuppofing rufticity, illiteracy, and
meanness, to be characteriftics of a
Gofpel church ; yet I may venture to
affert, that an affembly of princes in a
fplendid cathedral, with an archprelate
appearing in canonical pomp, may in-
fult the Divine Majefty, and be utterly
unworthy the name of a church ; while
a congregation of day-labourers, with
an illiterate minister in the meaneft ha-
bit, convened in a barn, may be a fpiritual temple, enjoy the Divine Prefence,·
and perform the Chriftian worfhip in
all its glory.--It has been well obferved, by a certain author, that " the
" prefence of God confers dignity and
" importance :" but that " he can re-
" ceive none from created, much lefs
" from artificial pomp and magnifi-
" cence." To which I will add, in
the words of Dr. Owen; " If the whole
" ftructure of the temple, and all its
" beautiful fervices, were now in be-
" ing on the earth, no glory would re-
" dound unto God thereby : he would
" receive none from it. To expect the

" glory of God in them, would be an
" high difhonor unto him*."

If fecular grandeur, however, muft
needs attend the religion of Him who
was born in a ftable, and lived in poverty, who received the acclamations of
royalty, when riding upon an afs, and
quickly after expired on a crofs ;--if,
I fay, it *muft* appear in the worfhip of
any who pretend to follow the Fifher-
men of Galilee, thofe prime minifters
in the Mefliah's kingdom, let it be confined to fuch as avow themfelves members of a National eftablifhment. For,
with regard to thofe who maintain that
particular churches are Congregational, confifting of fuch as make a credible
profeffion of repentance and faith ;
pomp and fhow in the worfhip of God
are quite unbecoming their principles.
Yes, let thofe monopolize the fplendor
in queftion, who confider the church
and the ftate as of equal dimenfions ;
who acknowledge a vifible head of political royalty ; and who muft fearch,
not the New Teftament, but a code of
Canons and Conftitutions larger than

* *On the Perfon of Chrift*, p. 354, 355.

the whole Bible*, if they would know on what foundations their ecclefiafti- cal fabric ftands, and by what laws it is governed. The National form of the Jewifh church being their model, and a temporal monarch being their head, why fhould not they have magnificent cathedrals, and confecrate them like Jewifh temples? Why fhould not anci- ent Judaifm be imitated in thefe parti- culars, as well as in other things? As the head of the Englifh Church is adorned with royal robes; as the prin- ciple officers in it are appointed by him, and are Lords in the legiflature; and as it is eftablifhed by laws of the ftate, who fhall forbid the various orders of its minifters being adorned with found- ing titles, and with pompous canoni- cals? There is no reafon to wonder that, in fuch a conftitution and fuch a polity, almoft every thing fhould wear a fecular appearance. For, political

* Refering to *Gibfon's Codex*. " When," fays Sir *Michael Forfter*, " Chriftianity became the " eftablifhed religion of the empire, and church " and ftate became one body, confidered only " in different views and under different relations ; " the ecclefiaftical and civil laws of the empire " flowed from one and the fame fource, *imperial* " *refcripts*." *Examinat. of Bp. Gibfon's Codex, p.* 122. Edit. 3d.

authority pervading the whole eccleſiaſtical frame, it would be inconſiſtent
with itſelf if its various parts had not an
air of external grandeur. As a kingdom of this world, it is reſpectable ;
but it ſhould not pretend to any thing
more.

But, however it may be with a National eſtabliſhment, let not Proteſtant
Diſſenters behave as if they envied, either its magnificence, or its emoluments. No : let not thoſe who conſider the Church and the World as oppo-
ſite ideas ; who maintain, that Chriſt
only is the head of Chriſtian communities ; and that the New Teſtament con-
tains the whole of their eccleſiaſtical polity, be deſirous of external grandeur
in any thing pertaining to public worſhip : leſt they practically deny their
own principles, and implicitly reproach
primitive Chriſtianity for being too
ſimple and too ſpiritual. It is frequently much eaſier for people, and
much more deſired by them, to aſſemble
in an elegant edifice, and for their miniſter to appear in canonical faſhion ;
than to perform a ſpiritual worſhip, and
to ſhine in the beauties of holineſs. The

fplendor of a place for affembling, and the pageantry of clerical drefs, are procured by money; but the graces of real fanctity, and internal devotion, are of heavenly origin: nor is the exercife of them to be expected, unlefs by thofe who are habitually aiming at it.--I will add, whatever kind of fucceffion to the Apoftles may be claimed by diocefan bifhops*, yet let not Proteftant Diffenting minifters implicitly arrogate an apoftolic miffion, powers, and authority, by calling themfelves AMBASSADORS *of Chrift*. For that character, it is plain, belonged to the firft-rate meffengers of our divine Sovereign Or, if any of thofe who publifh the gofpel of peace confider a title of that high importance as quite fuitable to the dignity of their ecclefiaftical ftation, their credentials muft be produced.

By this characteriftic of our Lord's kingdom, and by the general nature of it, we are further taught, That *fimplicity* and *fpirituality* muft conftitute the chief glory of that worfhip which he requires ---This forms another ftriking defparity between the Meffiah's government and

* See Dr. Owen's *Nature of a Gofpel Church, and its Government*. p. 33.

the ancient Theocracy.---It has been obferved, by Dr. ERSKINE, that " the " refpect paid to God, under the Old " Teftament Difpenfation, correfpond- " ed to his character as a temporal mo- " narch ; and in a great meafure con- " fifted in external pomp and gaiety, " dancing, inftrumental mufic, and " other expreffions of joy ufual at co- " ronations or triumphs. But the hour " is now come, in which the true " worfhippers muft worfhip the Fa- " ther in fpirit and in truth ; not with " external fhow and pageantry*." Yes, numerous rites, and ceremonious pomp, were appointed by Jehovah in the firft eftablifhment of the Jewifh church : to which various additions were made, by divine order, in the time of David†. Thefe things were undoubtedly fuited to the nature of that Difpenfation, and to the church of God, while in a ftate of minority‡. On worfhip, fo various in its branches, and fo fplendid in its ap- pearance, multitudes attended, and found amufement in it, who were in their hearts difaffected to God. In hearing the temple mufic, vocal and in- ftrumental, there is no doubt but num-

* *Theological Differtations*, p. 69.   † 1 Chron. xvi. 4, 5, 6.   2 Chron. xxix. 25.   ‡ Gal. iv. 1--7.

bers of ungodly people were much de-.
lighted. Such a concert, by perfons.
trained to the employment, and under,
the direction of fkilful mafters, muft.
produce very pleafing emotions in the;
attending multitude : a great majority,
of whom, it is highly probable, confi-.
dered their fyftem of worfhip as the beft,
that could be appointed, it being fo,
grand and fo delightful.

But though that fyftem was fitted both;
to the people, and to the times; though,
it was of great utility, and anfwered the
purpofe of Jehovah, under a fhadowy
difpenfation; yet the New Teftament,
informs us, that its numerous rites were,
the mere *elements* of fpiritual know-.
ledge, and of holy worfhip. Nay, compared with appointments and fervices;
of the Chriftian church, that they were,
beggarly elements and *carnal* ordinances*.-- Why, then, fhould any profeffors of Chriftianity be fo fond of ceremonious pomp in the worfhip of God?
Why fo attached to the language and
forms of Judaifm, or practife a ritual.
nearly akin to the rubrics of Mofes ?
Why call the holy fupper a *facrifice*,.
the Lord's table an *altar*, and the ad-.

* Gal. iv. 9. Heb. ix. 10.

miniftrator a *prieft*? Why have re-
courfe to the temple worfhip for mufical inftruments, and for a fet of fingers
diftinct from the congregation at large?
Why fhould refponfive finging, and
tunes more fit for a theatre than for the
worfhip of God, be heard in religious
affemblies? Why, without an appointment for alternate finging, fhould one
part of a congregation fufpend an act
of focial worfhip, while the other car-
ries it on? To thefe and fimilar que-
ries the anfwer muft be; Becaufe things
of this nature amufe and pleafe the carnal mind--Becaufe the fimplicity and
fpirituality of New Teftament worfhip
have no charms for the multitude---
And becaufe the generality love to perform fomething called *religious worfhip*,
in a way of their own devifing. To
fave appearances, however, as many
things in the Jewifh ritual were pretty
well adapted to pleafe the carnally
minded, they will be contented with
having the Chriftian worfhip reformed,
in various particulars, according to the
ancient model, as completed in the time
of David.--Who, that enters a fplendid edifice, where he beholds a minifter in his canonicals, and meets with
fuch entertaining worfhip, can forbear

to think of the temple fervice ? Such,
through a courfe of ages, has been the
predilection of multitudes for ancient
Judaifm, that a number of its peculiarities, which were either honorable
and profitable to the priefts, or amufing
and pleafing to the people, have been
incorporated with Chriftianity, notwithftanding the mifchiefs produced
by fimilar conduct in the apoftolic
churches.

I faid, *Honorable and profitable* to the
priefts--- *Amufing and pleafing* to the
people. But here they ftop : for thofe
branches of Judaifm that were of a different kind, are treated as entirely obfolete. So, for inftance, though numbers of Chriftian minifters are fond
enough of prieftly veftments, and of
tithes, *jure divino* ; yet they are not inclined always to *wafh their feet*, before
they perform facred fervice* ; much
lefs to perform it *barefoot*† --As to the
people, though multitudes of them are
greatly delighted with pompous appearances and mufical founds, they are
far from being in raptures with *circum-*

---

* Exod. xxx. 17---21.   † See Dr. Lightfoot's
Temple Service, Chap. I and X. and Dr. Gill on
Exod. iii. 5.

cifion. For notwithftanding that A-
brahamic rite retained its obligation
and utility, as long as any Jewifh cere-
mony did; and though, in apoftolic
times, judaizing Chriftians had the
higheft opinion of its importance; yet,
like the ancient baptifmal immerfion, it
is now confidered as too painful and
too indelicate for polifhed perfons to
regard.--Thus the worfhip of the New
Oeconomy is become a compound, unknown to the Bible, of Judaifm and
Chriftianity: and it is treated by too
many minifters, as a trade, not a divine
fervice; by numbers of people, as an
article of decent amufement fuitable to
the Lord's day, not as duty to God, and
as a mean of preparing for heaven.
" Men run to church, fays ERASMUS,
" as to a theatre, to have their ears
" tickled*." *The prophets prophefy
falfely, and the priefts bear rule by their
means, and my people love to have it fo:
and what will ye do in the end thereof?*†

But though the magnificence of places intended for public worfhip, the
confecration of thofe places, canonical
habits, and various amufing ceremonies are *now* defended (if defended at

* In 1 Cor. xiv. 19.   † Jer. v. 31.

all by Scripture) on the ground of Old
Teſtament cuſtoms; yet we are taught
by the moſt reſpectable eccleſiaſtical
hiſtorians, that they originated in a per-
verſe imitation of Paganiſm. Chriſtians being ſurrounded with Heathens,
of whoſe converſion they were deſirous; and the latter having been accuſ-
tomed, in performing their idolatrous
worſhip, to the external pomp of temples and of ceremonies; CONSTAN-
TINE had no ſooner aboliſhed the ſu-
perſtitions of his anceſtors, than magnificent places of worſhip were erected,
and conſecrated with great parade: it
being conſidered as unlawful, except
in extraordinary caſes, to perform any
part of public worſhip in them, previous to their conſecration. Heathens
having often reproached Chriſtianity,
for the poverty and ſimplicity of its appearance, the Chriſtians of the fourth
century adopted many of the Pagan
rites. Miniſters of the word, for example, when performing their office,
appeared in canonical habits, and with
prieſtly pomp. Their newly erected
temples were conſecrated, by ſinging
of ſuch hymns as were thought ſuita-
ble to the occaſion, by prayers, and by
thankſgivings. Then, in the Eaſtern

churches, the refponfive finging of David's Pfalms was introduced ; precentors were appointed, and laws were framed by different Councils to direct the fingers in the performance of their fervice*.--Such was the origin of thofe gaudy appearances which, to amufe the carnal mind, have fo long corrupted the worfhip of God, and fecularized the kingdom of Chrift ! *Vain man would be wife*, and, in his great wifdom, thinks it neceffary to add a few ornaments and fupports to this heavenly empire, of which it was entirely deftitute when the Apoftles left the earth. This was thought expedient, in order to render the religion of Jefus a little more pleafing, refpectable, and edifying, than it was in its native ftate. But well may he demand, with the afpect of incenfed majefty, *Who hath required this at your hand?*

The kingdom of Chrift is not of this world, in refpect of its immunities, its riches, and its honors. Wealth, titles, and authority, are frequently confered by fecular princes : but they are all external

I

---

* Vid. *Spanhemii Hift. Ecclef* Secul. IV. p. 851, 854. *Venema Hift. Ecclef.* Secul. IV. § 128.

things. A patent of peerage, or a lucrative office, gives no wifdom to the mind, no peace to the confcience, no holinefs to the heart. The poffoffor, notwithftanding his plentiful income and fplendid title, may be a fool, a wretch, and a difgrace to the human fpecies.--The higheft honors and the greateft emoluments which the fubjects of an earthly kingdom can enjoy, are all of them unfatisfactory : and, therefore, the firft favourites of temporal princes are fometimes the moft unhappy. Of this we have a remarkable inftance in Haman, the prime favourite of Ahafuerus.--Great privileges and exalted honors are enjoyed by comparatively very few fubjects of any temporal monarch ; the nature of the cafe forbidding them to become general, among the inhabitants of any country. Dukedoms, marquifates, and grants from the crown, are but feldom beftowed, how loyal foever the fubjects may be. Befides, thofe diftinguifhed favors are of fhort duration, and quite uncertain.

Whereas, the immunities, emoluments, and honors of our Lord's kingdom, are all of them fpiritual and internal. They are fuited to the ftate of an enlightened mind, to the feelings of an awakened confcience, and to the defires of a renewed heart. Pardon of all fin, and complete acceptance with God; adoption into the heavenly family, and a title of future glory, are fome of the privileges and honors enjoyed by the fubjects of this kingdom. Bleflings, thefe, of infinite worth, becaufe of their fpiritual nature and immortal duration. Nor are they confined to a few diftinguifhed favourites of our celeftial Sovereign ; for they are common to all his real fubjects. Yes, they are all enriched, and all ennobled, with *rightcoufnefs, peace, and joy in the Holy Ghoft.*

Now, as the immunities, grants, and honors, beftowed by the King Mefliah, are all of a fpiritual nature ; his faithful fubjects have no reafon to wonder, or to be difcouraged, at any perfecutions, afflictions, or poverty which may befal them. Were his empire *of this world,* then indeed it might be expected, from the goodnefs of his heart and the power of his arm, that thofe who are fubmiffive to his authority, zealous for his honor, and conformed to his image, would commonly find themfelves eafy and profperous in their temporal circumſtances. Yes, were his dominion of a ſecular kind, it might be ſuppoſed that an habitually conſci- entious regard to his laws, would ſe- cure from the oppreſſion of ungodly men, and from the diſtreſſes of temporal want.--Thus it was with Iſrael under their Theocracy. When the rulers and the people in general were punctu- al in obſerving Jehovah's appoint- ments, the ſtipulations of the Sinai Co- venant ſecured them from being op- preſſed by their enemies, and from any remarkable affliction by the immediate hand of God. Performing the condi- tions of their National Confederation, they were, as a people, warranted to expect every ſpecies of temporal proſ- perity. Health, and long life, riches, honors, and victory over their enemies, were promiſed by Jehovah to their ex- ternal obedience*. The puniſhments alſo, that were denounced againſt fla- grant breaches of the Covenant made at Horeb, were of a temporal kind†.

---

* See Exod. xv. 25, 26. xxiii. 25--28. Lev. xxvi. 3--14. Deut. vii. 12--24. viii, 7. 8, 9. xi. 13--17. xxviii. 3--13.   † Lev. xxvi. 14--39. Deut. iv. 25, 26, 27. xi. 27. xxviii. 15--68. xxix. 22--28. See Dr. *Erſkine's Theolog. Diſſertat.* p. 22--29. *External* obedience---Puniſhments of a

In this refpect, however, as well as
in other things, there is a vaft difference
between the Jewifh, and the Chriftian
Oeconomy. This difparity was plainly intimated, if I miftake not, by the op-
pofite modes of divine proceeding, in
eftablifhing Jehovah's kingdom among
the Jews, and in founding the empire of
Jefus Chrift. To fettle the Ifraelitifh
church, to exalt the chofen tribes above
furrounding nations, and to render the
ancient Theocracy fupremely venera-
ble, the divine Sovereign appeared in
terrible majefty. Wafting plagues and
awful deaths were often inflicted by
eternal juftice, on thofe who dared to
oppofe, or to opprefs, the people of
God. An angel was commiflioned to
deftroy the Egyptian firft-born; Pha-
raoh, with his mighty hoft, were
drowned in the Red fea; and the Ca-
naanitifh nations were put to the fword,

I 2

temporal kind. Thefe and fimilar expreflions in
this Eflay are to be underftood, as referring to the
Sinai Covenant *ftrictly* confidered, and to Jehovah's
requifitions as the *king* of Ifrael. They are quite
confiftent, therefore, with its being the duty of A-
braham's natural feed to perform *internal* obedience to that Sublime Sovereign, confidered as God
of the whole earth; and with final punifhment being inflicted by him, in failure of that obedience.

that the subjects of Jehovah might poffefs their fertile country. Manifeft in-
dications thefe, in connection with ex-
prefs promifes, that the fpecial Providence of God would exalt and blefs the
natural feed of Abraham with temporal
felicity; provided they did not violate
the Sinai Covenant.

But when the Prince Meffiah founded his kingdom, all things were otherwife. No marks of external grandeur
attendeded his perfonal appearance :
and, inftead of executing righteous
vengeance on thofe who oppofed him,
his language was; *The Son of man is
not come to deftroy men's lives, but to fave
them. Father, forgive them, for they
know not what they do!*---After a life of
labour and of beneficence, of poverty
and of reproach, he fell a victim to perfecution, and a martyr to truth. Such
was the plan of divine Providence,
refpecting Chrift our King, and fuch
was the treatment with which he met
from the world! Striking intimations,
thofe, that his moft faithful fubjects
would have no ground of difcourage-
ment, in any fufferings which might
await them; and that, confidered as his
dependants, fpiritual bleffings were all
they fhould have to expect.

It muſt indeed be acknowledged, that as vicious tempers and immoral practices have a natural tendency to impair health, diſtreſs the mind, and waſte the property; ſo the exerciſe of holy affections, and the practice of true godlineſs, have the moſt friendly aſpect on a Chriſtian's own temporal happineſs, (except ſo far as perſecution intervenes) and on the welfare of ſociety. But then it is evident that this ariſes from the nature of things, and from the ſuperintendency of common Providence; rather than from the dominion of Chriſt, as a ſpiritural monarch. For, ſo conſidered, ſpiritual bleſſings are all that they have to expect from his royal hand.

By the prophetic declarations of our Lord himſelf, and by the hiſtory of this kingdom, it plainly appears, that among all the ſubjects of his government, none have been more expoſed to perſecution, affliction, and poverty, than thoſe who were moſt eminent for obedience to his laws, and moſt uſeful in his empire. The moſt uniform ſubjection to his authority, and the warmeſt zeal for his honor, that ever appeared upon earth; were no ſecurity from bitter perſecution, from pincking po-

verty, or from complicated affliction.
Our divine Lord, confidered as a fpiritual fovereign, is concerned for the fpiritual interefts of thofe that are under
his government. His perfonal perfections and royal prorogatives, his power and wifdom, his love and care, are
therefore to be regarded as engaged,
both by office and by promife,--not to
make his dependants eafy and profperous in their temporal concerns ; but--
to ftrengthen them for their fpiritual
warfare ; to preferve them from finally falling by their invible enemies; to
make all afflictions *work together for
their good*; to render them, in the final
iffue, *more than conquerors* over every
oppofer ; and to crown them with
everlafting life.

Our Lord has promifed, indeed, that
their obedience to his royal pleafure,
fhall meet with his gracious regards in
the prefent life. Not by indulging
them with temporal riches, or by
granting them external honor and eafe;
but by admitting them into more intimate communion with himfelf, and by
rejoicing their hearts with his favor*.
Yes, to deliver from fpiritual enemies,

* Joh. xii. 26. and xiv. 21, 23.

and to provide for spiritual wants ; to indulge with spiritual riches, and to ennoble with spiritual honors, are those royal acts which belong to Him, whose *kingdom is not of this world.* In the bestowment of these blessings, the glory of his regal character is much concerned. But millions of his devoted subjects may fall by the iron hand of oppression, starve in obscurity, or suffer accumulated affliction in other ways ; without the least impeachment of his power, his goodness, or his care, as the sovereign of a spiritual kingdom.

The kingdom of Christ is not like the dominions of secular princes, with regard to its limits and its duration. The widely extended monarchies of antiquity were confined to certain parts of the habitable globe, and in the course of a few centuries they came to an end. Not so, the empire of Jesus Christ : for thus run the prophetic oracles, respecting him and his kingdom. *He shall have dominion from sea to sea, and from the river to the ends of the earth. All things shall fall down before him : all nations shall serve him. There was given him dominion, and glory, and a kingdom, that all people, nations, and languages should serve him*. *His dominion is an everlasting dominion, which shall not pass away, and his kingdom that which shall not be destroyed. He shall reign over the house of Jacob for ever, and of his kingdom there shall be no end**. Concerning the gradual enlargement and universal extent of this kingdom, our Lord speaks in his parable of *a grain of mustard seed*; and in that of *leaven*, pervading the whole mass of meal.--This holy empire shall issue in the ultimate glory : and tho' the present form of its administration will cease, when *God shall be all in all*, yet the glorified subjects of it shall never die, never be disunited, nor ever withdraw their allegiance from Jesus Christ. Such are the foundations of his dominion, and such the excellence of his government, that each of his real subjects will from the heart say; LET THE KING LIVE ! *and let him reign, till all his enemies become his footstool*†!

Once more ; *The empire of Christ, or the Gospel Church, is called* THE KINGDOM OF HEAVEN. As our Lord, in the most emphatical manner, is denominated, THE KING OF KINGS ; we may with

---

* Pf. lxxii. 8. 11. Dan. vii 14. Luke i. 33.
† Pf. lxxii. 15. and c. 1. 1. Cor. xv. 25.

propriety confider his holy monarchy, as *the kingdom of kingdoms.* This appellation, *the kingdom of heaven*, manifeftly fets the New Teftament church at the greateft diftance from every fecular monarchy, and teaches us to confider it as nearly allied to the heavenly ftate*. The fubjects of it are defcribed, as born from above ; as the heirs of glory. They are governed by laws, indulged with privileges, and invefted with honors, which are entirely fpiritual, and all from heaven. The truths they believe, the bleffings they enjoy, the obedience they perform, and the expectations they entertain, have a regard to heaven. It is the authority of a divine Sovereign under which they live, and his approbation at which they aim. The pleafures which they enjoy, confidered as the fubjects of Jefus Chrift, are all of a fpiritual nature, and all favour of the heavenly world.

As Chrift is a fpiritual monarch, his dominion refpects the underftandings, the confciences, the hearts of men ;

* Ecclefiam Chrifti Jefu vere effe *Regnum Cælorum* et inter ejus ftatum et conditionem ecclefiæ cœleftis maximam intercedere affinitatem et conjunctionem. *Vitringa in Apocalypf.* p. 885. Amftalod. 1719.

and is a preparation for that fublime
ftate, where knowledge and rectitude,
where obedience and love, where harmony and joy, are all in their full glory.
The foundation of this government,
as it refpects individuals, is laid in regeneration.. There the preparation for
heaven begins: and all the genuine
fruits of that important change, which
is made by divine influence, in the
mind, confcience, and heart of a finner, have a tendency toward heaven;
and many of them are anticipations of
it. That worfhip which is performed
by the fubjects of Chrift, is no further
fpiritual, and agreeable to the New
Oeconomy, than it is animated with
fuch affections as abound in heaven.
For the time is come, when thofe that
worfhip the Father, *muft worfhip him in
fpirit and in truth.* Knowledge and
reverence of God, as revealed by the
Mediator; confidence in him, and love
to him; felf-abafement in his prefence,
and acquiefcence in his dominion; are
the principle ideas included in fpiritual
worfhip, whether as performed by the
fubjects of Chrift here, or by the faints
made perfect in glory.

It is manifest from this characteristic
of our Lord's kingdom, that a profeſſion of allegiance to him is entirely vain,
not attended with *fpiritual mindedneſs* :
becauſe it is natural for good ſubjects
to feek the profperity of that kingdom
to which they belong. Now the intereſts of Meſſiah's empire are all of a
ſpiritual nature. In the ſpread of evangelical truth, and the purity of divine
worſhip ; in the exerciſe of love, and
the practice of holineſs, the intereſts and
honor of this kingdom chiefly confiſt.
Indifference about thefe, is an evidence
of the heart being difaffected to our divine Sovereign ; but allegiance to him,
will manifeſt itſelf by an habitual regard to them.--In whomſoever this
holy Monarch reigns, there is a reliſh
for ſpiritual riches, honors, pleaſures.
To enjoy his favor, and bear his
image ; to perform his will, and behold his glory, are things of the higheſt importance in the eſteem of real
faints. Nor is it a mere dictate of the
underſtanding and conſcience, that it
ſhould be fo. It is matter of choice :
for their hearts are engaged on thoſe
objects.

K

It is common for subjects to imitate a sovereign whom they love and revere ; elpeceially, if they have derived signal benefits from his adminiftration. Now such is the nature of our Lord's government, that it is impoffible for any one to be under it, without fincerely loving and profoundly revering him--without feeing an excellence in his example, which commands elteem and excites imitation. But if we be fond of wealth, or emulous of grandeur and fhow ; if we purfue preeminence, and grafp at power; we imitate the children of this world, not Jefus Chrift. Thofe things are eagerly fought, and highly prized, by the fubjects of Satan, becaufe they are carnally minded ; but he is unworthy to be called a difciple of Chrift, who is not habitually ftriving to copy his example. Nor can any pretend, that he ever encouraged, by word or deed, the purfuit of fecular diftinctions, the acquifition of wealth, or the pleafures of fenfuality, but quite the reverfe. Far from feeking *honor which comes from men*, he neither courted the fmiles of the rich, nor the patronage of the mighty : for *the friendſhip of this world, is enmity with God:* So our Lord efteemed it, and fo muſt his diſciples. To be the ſubjeɕts of a ſpiritual kingdom, and to have our hearts on temporal enjoyments, are inconſiſtent. *To be carnally minded is death; but to be ſpiritually minded, is life and peace.*

As Chriſt is a ſpiritual ſovereign, and his church a ſpiritual kingdom, all the ſubjeɕts of his government muſt be conſidered, as *in a ſtate of preparation for heaven.* The prevailing diſpoſitions of their hearts are in favor of heavenly things · and to promote the exerciſe of ſpiritual affeɕtions, the New Oeconomy, in all its branches, is much better adapted than was the Moſaic ſyſtem. For as it is the moſt perfeɕt diſpenſation of divine grace, that ever was, or ever will be enjoyed on earth; ſo it makes the neareſt approaches to heaven.

It has been juſtly remarked by a certain author, "That the Legal Oeco-
" nomy introduced that of Grace, by
" the goſpel, and then vaniſhed away.
" The Diſpenſation of Grace, in like
" manner, is now performing its work,
" fulfilling its day, announcing, un-
" folding, introducing the kingdom
" of glory: and *when that which is per-*

" *fe&t is come, then that which is in part*
" *fhall be done away.*"--Yes, the Old
Oeconomy, and the Jewifh Theocracy,
were manifeftly introductory to the
Chriftian Difpenfation, and the Meffiah's kingdom. Thofe, being typical
and fhadowy, led to thefe, and in them
received their final completion. But
the New Difpenfation, and the kingdom of Chrift, have no completion
fhort of heaven. Thither they lead,
and there they terminate. No worfhip is agreeable to the Mefliah's kingdom, which is not animated by heavenly affections. All the external fervices of religion are only fo many
means of exciting thofe holy affections, of promoting communion with
God, and of cultivating a heavenly
temper. Confequently, the worfhip of
thofe who reft in exterior fervices, is
quite fuperficial, and has nothing fpiritual, nothing heavenly in it.

Jehovah, under the former Difpenfation, having chofen the Holy of holies
for the place of his refidence, the Jews
were directed to addrefs him in prayer,
confidered as on his throne *between the*

Cherubim*. They knew, indeed, that he inhabited celeſtial manſions ; and therefore, when bending the knee before him, their hands were extended toward heaven† : but yet he was more immediately regarded by them, as reſiding in the earthly ſanctuary. For, notwithſtanding their deſire to be heard in *heaven*, " the cry of their prayer, " and the eye of their faith, were di- " rected firſt to the *mercyſeat*." The moſt eminent ſaints, under that Occonomy, looked to God in both ; did homage to him in both ; nor could they have neglected him in reſpect of either, without being culpable.---Whereas, when Chriſtians pray, they look directly to their *Father who is in heaven*, and as on a throne of grace in the celeſtial temple ; without the leaſt regard to any place upon earth, or to any viſible object‡.

" God, ſays Dr ERSKINE, as huſband " of the the Goſpel church, claims " from his people inward affection and " love, and accepts them only who

K 2

---

* 1 Kings viii. 27--30, 38, 42, 44, 49. 2 Kings xix. 15. Pſalm xxviii. 2. lxxx. 1 Dan. vi. 10.
† 1 Kings viii. 22. ‡ See Dr. *Goodwin on Chriſt the Mediator*, B. VI. Chap. iii.

" worfhip him in fpirit and in truth. In
" the mofaic covenant it was otherwife.
" There he appeared chiefly as a tem-
" poral prince, and therefore gave laws
" intended rather to direct the outward
" conduct, than to regulate the actings
" of the heart. Hence every thing in
" that Difpenfation was adapted to
" ftrike his fubjects with awe and re-
" verence. The magnificence of his
" palace, and all its utenfils; his nu-
" merous train of attendants; the
" fplendid robes of the high-prieft,
" who, though his prime minifter, was
" not allowed to enter the Holy of ho-
" lies, fave once a year, and, in all his
" miniftrations, was obliged to difco-
" ver the moft humble veneration for
" Ifrael's King; the folemn rites with
" which the priefts were confecrated;
" the ftrictnefs with which all impuni-
" ties and indecencies were forbidden,
" as things which, though tolerable in
" others, were unbecoming the dig-
" nity of the people of God, efpecially
" when approaching to him : all thefe
" tended to promote and fecure the
" refpect due to their glorious Sove-
" reign."--It was, however, foretold,
by one of the minor Prophets, " that
" in Gofpel times, men fhould not call

" God, *Baali*. i. e. *my Mafter*, but *Ifhi*.
" i. e. *my Hufband*--The paffage im-
" ports at leaft thus much, that God,
" who in the Jewifh Difpenfation had
" chiefly difplayed the grandeur, dif-
" tance, and feverity of a Mafter,
" would, in the Chriftian Difpenfati-
" on, chiefly difplay the affection and
" familiarity of a hufband and friend*."

Yes, under the Mofaic fyftem, the highprieft only, and he but once in a year, was admitted to the mercyfeat, or throne of Jehovah, in *a worldly fanc-tuary*. That appearance of the Jewifh pontiff before the Lord, though grand and folemn, was a mere emblem of fpi-ritual things, and of that holy inter-courfe which all the fubjects of this kingdom have with God, in the per-formance of fpiritual worfhip. For as Jefus entered into the heavenly fanctu-ary, *with his own blood :* as he is there *a prieft upon his throne*, uniting the fa-cerdotal cenfer with the regal ceptre ; he ever lives, not only to govern his widely extended empire, but likewife to intercede for all his followers, and to be the medium of their accefs to the di-vine Father. In virtue of his atone-

* *Theological Differtations*, p. 4, 5, 6

ment made on the crofs, and of his appearance in the heavenly world, the meaneſt ſubjects of his dominion, when performing ſacred ſervice, *have boldneſs to enter into the holieſt*. Each of them, in the exerciſe of faith, of hope, and of love, has acceſs to the Divine Majeſty on a throne of grace ; and each has reaſon to expect a condeſcending audience from the King Eternal. Hence we find, that New Teſtament ſaints are called *the domeſtics of God* ; which " "may have ſome relation to that " peculiar nearneſs to God, in which " the Jewiſh prieſts were : and refer " to that great intimacy of unreſtrain- " ed converſe to which we, as Chriſti- " ans, are admitted. In which reſ- " pect our privileges ſeem to reſemble, " not only thoſe of the people praying " in the *common court* of Iſrael ; but of " the prieſts, worſhipping in the *houſe* " *itſelf**."

The ſuperior advantages of believers under the Chriſtian Oeconomy, in regard to communion with God, and the ſanctifying influence which that holy intercourſe has on their minds, are ſtrongly expreſſed in the following re-

* Dr. *Doddridge's Note*, on Epheſ. ii. 19.

markable words : *But we all, IN an unveiled face, beholding as in a glafs the
glory of the Lord, are changed into the
fame image, from glory to glory, even as
by the Spirit of the Lord**. The Apof-
tle here plainly alludes to that glory
which appeared in the face of Mofes,
after his intimate converfe with Jehovah on the mount. So dazzling was
the luftre of his countenance, that the
children of Ifrael *were afraid to come
nigh him.* He therefore put a veil upon his face, that they might have fami-
liar intercourfe with him† : which veil
was an emblem, not only of the Jewifh
blindednefs, but alfo of the darknefs of
that Difpenfation.--Now, in contraft
with thefe things, Paul informs us, that
the glory of the divine perfections appears and fhines in the *unveiled* face of
Jefus Chrift; that this glory is *beheld*

* 2 Cor. iii. 18. *In an unveiled face.* So, I
humbly conceive, fhould here be rendered. Com-
pare 2 Cor. iv. 6. where the infpired writer fpeaks
of *the light of the knowledge of the glory of God,
in the face of Jefus Chrift.* That will admit the
fupplemental prepofition *in*, as well as *with*, cannot,
I prefume, be doubted : and that the whole fcope
of Paul's reafoning in the context leads us to think
of the face of *Chrift*, rather than that of *believers*,
being *unveiled*, is, if I miftake not, folidly proved by
the learned *Ikenius*, in his *Diſſertat. Philolog. Theolog.* Diſſert. xxvi. § 4, 5, 6. † Exod. xxxiv. 29. 35.

by New Testament believers; and that, by beholding it, they are gradually *transformed into the glorious image of God.* What an illustrious view does the Apostle here give us of the New Oeconomy! He not only represents the state and privileges of the Gospel Church, as greatly superior to those of the Jewish people; but as nearly approaching to the employments, and the fruitions of the celestial world. For we cannot easily form a more exalted idea of the business and blessedness of heaven, than that of contemplating the glory of God, and of making continual advances in likeness to him.

As, in the person of our Mediator, the nature of God and the nature of man were not united, till just before the commencement of this kingdom; as God was not *manifested in the flesh,* but with an immediate view to this holy and spiritual empire; so there is no reason to wonder that the favored subjects of Messiah's government have a more intimate communion with Jehovah, than was ever enjoyed by the Jewish church. Under the Old Covenant, Israel in general had a kind of local nearness to God, in the performance of religious worſhip ; and real ſaints had ſpiritual communion with him _ But then it was by means of prieſts, who had infirmities ; of ſacrifices, that were imperfect ; and of ſervices, that were mere ſhadows of heavenly things: all which were confined to an earthly ſanctuary. Whereas the ſubjects of Jeſus Chriſt have acceſs to the Father of mercies, without regarding any prieſt, beſides their Sovereign ; any ſacrifice, beſides his death; any incenſe, beſides his interceſſion. All theſe they regard as appearing, as operating, as efficacious on their behalf, in the heavenly ſanctuary. Yes, their High-prieſt, who is of infinite dignity ; their ſacrifice, which is of boundleſs worth ; and their incenſe, which is conſummately fragrant, are for ever in the immediate preſence of God--for ever deſerving, and for ever obtaining the divine approbation. On theſe, therefore, in all their approaches to Eternal Majeſty, their dependence fixes. Hence their worſhip is performed, through the aids of grace, with reverence and with confidence, with love and with delight. *We have acceſs with confidence, by the faith of* Chriſt.

Now, to worſhip God with profound reverence, yet without a ſlaviſh
fear; with ſteady confidence, connected with deep humility; with ſubmiſ-
ſion to his will, as the moſt high Lord;
with love to his excellence, as the infinite beauty; and with joy in his all-
ſufficiency, as the Chief Good; is to
perform a ſpiritual ſervice, and to adore
in a heavenly manner. In the performance of ſuch worſhip, we have communion with *the ſpirits of juſt men made
perfect*--we enter within the veil--we
have fellowſhip with God--we antici-
pate the buſineſs of heaven, and taſte
its refined pleaſures. In theſe holy ex-
erciſes of the mind, conſcience, and
heart, we feel ourſelves near to God,
as the fountain of all bleſſedneſs, and
are trained for the heavenly world.
Thus we are habituated to a kind of
celeſtial ſervice, by which our likeneſs
to Chriſt is promoted, and our deſires
after heaven increaſed. In theſe things
the very life of ſpiritual worſhip and of
real religion conſiſts. He therefore is
not worthy to be called a ſubject of
our Lord's kingdom, who is not habitually aiming in his devotional ſervices,
at his delightful and ſolemn intercourſe
with God. Nor is he deſerving of that

exalted character, whofe thoughts and cares, whofe hopes and fears, whofe joys and forrows, are not principally concerned about the government and grace of Chrift, confidered in their connection with the heavenly ftate.

It muft, indeed, be admitted, that this communion with heaven is extremely imperfect in the prefent life. Becaufe, though every true fubject of the King Meffiah be in a ftate very different from that of a merely nominal Chriftian, and though he is thankful for that difference ; yet he is not, he cannot be fatisfied, either with what he knows, or with what he enjoys ; with what he is, or with what he does. Not with what he *knows* : for he knows but *in part*, and he feels the deficiency. His acquaintance with the Greateft and Beft of beings--with the character and perfections, with the works and ways of God, is extremely fmall. His knowledge of the adorable Jefus--of his Perfon and offices, of his grace and work, of his kingdom and glory, is very contracted. Nay, the knowledge he has of himfelf, and of his final deftination in the heavenly world, is exceedingly

L

scanty : for *the heart is deceitful above all things ;* and *it does not yet appear what we shall be.* He cannot therefore be contented with such a pittance of spiritual knowledge.

Not with what he *enjoys :* for his enjoyment of spiritual pleasure is, at the highest, comparatively low. Besides, it is frequently interrupted by the insurrections of indwelling sin, and by the incursions of outward temptation. Though he sometimes exults in the light of God's countenance, partaking of joy that is *unspeakable and full of glory;* yet he frequently mourns the want of that exalted pleasure, and *groans being burdened.*

Not with what he *is :* for he feels much depravity, and laments over it, as affecting his mind with darkness; his conscience with guilt, or with stupidity ; and his passions with carnality. So far from perfectly bearing the image of Christ, that his language frequently is ; *O wretched man that I am ! who shall deliver me from the body of this death!*

Not with what he *does:* for though he sincerely desires to perform the will of God, as revealed in divine precepts, and illuftrated by the example of Chrift; yet he perceives that his obedience is very imperfect. Does he, for inftance, addrefs himfelf to God in prayer? in that devout exercife his whole foul fhould be engaged. Reverence of the divine Majefty, and an abafing fenfe of his own guilt; faith in the great atonement, and confidence in paternal mercy; the ardour of petition, and the comfort of expectation, fhould be all united. But frequently, alas! his thoughts wander, and his pious affections are dull, if not dormant. His prayer feems little befides a conflict with his own corruption. He rifes from his knees with forrow and with fighs. Afhamed of the manner in which he has treated the omnifcient Object of his worfhip, he cannot forbear exclaiming; *God be merciful to me a finner!* and this, perhaps, is the only petition over which he does not mourn, as deftitute of holy animation.--Or if he enjoy liberty in his converfe with the Father of all mercies, how often does he find fecret pride, and felf-gratulation, arife in his heart? as if the Moft Holy would regard his confeffions, petitions, and thankfgivings for the fake of their own excellence! Aware of the latent poifon, he is almoſt confounded. For well he knows, that Chriſtianity is the religion of ſinners--of depraved, of guilty, of unworthy creatures: and that nothing is more inconſiſtent with evangelical truth, or more deteſtable in the ſight of our Maker, than ſelf-applauſe reſpecting acceptance with God. Knowing himſelf to be a polluted worm that deſerves to periſh, he trembles to think of ever ſuppoſing that the majeſty of the Moſt High, and the purity of the Moſt Holy, will accept his imperfect ſervices for their own ſake. In the moſt emphatical manner he, therefore, with Job exclaims; *Behold, I am vile !--I abhor myſelf !* So various and ſo great are the defects in our devotional ſervices, that we might well deſpair, were it not for a High-prieſt who bears the iniquity of our *holy things.* For we *find a law, that when we would do good, evil is preſent with us.*

To ſuch imperfections and ſuch complaints, is a real ſubject of our Lord's dominion liable in the preſent life. But, looking forward to the ſeparate ſtate, when he ſhall *be with Chriſt, which is far better,* and to the reſurrection of the righteous ; with joy he adopts the language of David and fays, *I fhall be satisfied, when I awake with thy likeness.* Yes, when that ultimate and everlasting Oeconomy commences, his mind being all irradiated with divine truth, he shall be satisfied with what he *knows:* perfectly possessing the Chief Good, he shall be satisfied with what he *enjoys;* conscious of complete rectitude, he shall be satisfied with what he *is:* and knowing his obedience to be consummate, he shall be satisfied with what he *does.*--Delightful, ravishing thought! To have all our immortal powers expanded and filled, with knowledge of the Supreme truth, and with love to the Supreme Beauty; with reverence of the Supreme Lord, and with delight in the Supreme Good, must constitute complete happiness. Yet such is the grand result of our Lord's dominion in the hearts of men! To this, therefore, we must look, upon this our affections must be placed, if we would behave as the subjects of Jesus Christ, and finish our course with honor. For as this life is the seed-time of an eternal harvest; as no one *gathers grapes of thorns, or figs of thistles;* and as *whatever a man sows, that shall he also reap;* so we have no

L 2

reafon to expect heaven as our final refidence, if we be not habitually defirous
of communion with God in all our worfhip, and of making it our bufinefs to
perform his will.

It is one of the nobleft and moft delightful employments of the human
mind, to contemplate the gradual revelation of Jehovah's will, and the grow-
ing difplay of his eternal favor, from
the fall of our firft parents, to the con-
fummation of the divine Oeconomy.
It is both pleafing and improving to reflect on the Patriarchal Difpenfation introducing the Mofaic Syftem ; on the
Sinai Confederation making way for
the New Covenant ; on the Jewifh
Theocracy leading to thé Kingdom of
Chrift ; on the government of that
kingdom as a preparation for celeftial
manfions ; on the performance of holy
worfhip, by the fubjects of Chrift here,
as the mean of communion with *faints
in light* ; and on the prefent ftate of
worfhip and of bleffednefs in the heavenly fanctuary, as preparing for the
ultimate glory.

In reference to the communion of
believers with *the fpirits of juft men made*

perfect, in the performance of spiritual worship; and respecting the consummation of all things, Dr. OWEN speaks as follows, with whose words I shall conclude. " Were all that die in the " Lord immediately received into that " state wherein *God shall be all in all*, " without any use of the mediation of " Christ, or the worship of praise and " honor unto God by him, without be- " ing exercised in the ascription of ho- " nor, glory, power and dominion unto " [Christ,] on the account of the past " and present discharge of his office; " there could be no communion be- " tween them and us. But whilst they " are in the *sanctuary*, in *the temple of* " *God*, in the holy worship of Christ, " and of God in him, and we are not " only employed in the same work in " sacred ordinances suited unto our " state and condition, but in the per- " formance of our duties do by faith " *enter in within the veil*, and approach " unto the same throne of grace in the " most holy place; there is a spiritual " communion between them and us. " So the Apostle expresseth it, in the " twelfth of Hebrews--As we are here, " in and by the word and other ordi- " nances, prepared and made meet for

" the prefent ftate of things in glory;
" fo are they, : the fpirits of the juft
" made pertect] by the temple wor-
" fhip of heaven, fitted for that ftate of
" things when Chrift fhall *give up the,*
" *kingdom unto the Father, that* GOD
" MAY BE ALL IN ALL*."

* *On the Perfon of Chrift*, Chap. xx. p. 365, 366.

THOSE WHO WISH TO POSSESS
THE Rev. ABRAHAM BOOTHS'
PIECE ON *BAPTISM*, ARE IN-
FORMED, THEY MAY BE SUP-
PLIED IN THE SPRING, BY AP-
PLYING TO THE Rev. WILLIAM
ROGERS, OF PHILADELPHIA,---
AND BY Mr. SING, OF NEW-
YORK.-----*A L S O*----BOOTHS'
*REIGN OF GRAC*E.

www.ingramcontent.com/pod-product-compliance
Lightning Source LLC
Chambersburg PA
CBHW021138020726
47500CB00003B/1144